Global Sales

Leo Gough

- Fast-track route to new skills required in achieving global sales for any size of organization

- Covers the enormous growth potential offered by global sales, use of a local sales force, web selling, intellectual property and privacy, and standardization or adaptation of your products and services

- Case studies from Budweiser, Boo.com, McDonald's, Checkpoint and Samsung

- Includes a comprehensive resources guide, key concepts and thinkers, a 10-step action plan for achieving global sales, and a section of FAQs

SALES

12.02

>>EXPRESS EXEC.COM<<
essential management thinking at your fingertips

First Published 2003 by
Capstone Publishing Limited (a Wiley company)
8 Newtec Place
Magdalen Road
Oxford OX4 1RE
United Kingdom
http://www.capstoneideas.com

CIP catalogue records for this book are available from the British Library and the
US Library of Congress

ISBN 1-84112-455-9

Wiley also publishes its books in a variety of electronic formats. Some content
that appears in print may not be available in electronic books.

Websites often change their contents and addresses; details of sites listed in this
book were accurate at the time of writing, but may change.

Substantial discounts on bulk quantities of Capstone Books are available to
corporations, professional associations and other organizations. For details
telephone Capstone Publishing on (+44-1865-798623), fax (+44-1865-
240941) or email (info@wiley-capstone.co.uk).

Contents

Introduction to ExpressExec

ExpressExec is a completely up-to-date resource of current business practice, accessible in a number of ways – anytime, anyplace, anywhere. ExpressExec combines best practice cases, key ideas, action points, glossaries, further reading, and resources.

Each module contains 10 individual titles that cover all the key aspects of global business practice. Written by leading experts in their field, the knowledge imparted provides executives with the tools and skills to increase their personal and business effectiveness, benefiting both employee and employer.

ExpressExec is available in a number of formats:

» **Print** – 120 titles available through retailers or printed on demand using any combination of the 1200 chapters available.
» **E-Books** – e-books can be individually downloaded from ExpressExec.com or online retailers onto PCs, handheld computers, and e-readers.
» **Online** – http://www.expressexec.wiley.com/ provides fully searchable access to the complete ExpressExec resource via the Internet – a cost-effective online tool to increase business expertise across a whole organization.

» **ExpressExec Performance Support Solution (EEPSS)** – a software solution that integrates ExpressExec content with interactive tools to provide organizations with a complete internal management development solution.
» **ExpressExec Rights and Syndication** – ExpressExec content can be licensed for translation or display within intranets or on Internet sites.

To find out more visit www.ExpressExec.com or contact elound@wiley-capstone.co.uk.

Introduction

» What makes global sales different?

"The key thing is not just to plant flags. It's to make sure you build a business, customer by customer, day by day."
Peter M. Thompson, CEO, PepsiCo Beverages International

Why should selling abroad be any different from selling at home? Finding prospects, identifying their needs, demonstrating the product, explaining the features and benefits, and getting to a close are well-established universal techniques, aren't they? A moment's thought will show why this may not be so; in our home market, we can identify many factors over which we have no control – a new law, a change in fashion, a major strike, regulations, new technology, and the climate and topography of the country all affect the selling job, and companies must adapt to the prevailing conditions. The same is true abroad – most countries in the world have a unique set of conditions to which a firm must adapt. While objectives and essential techniques of selling remain the same, an international sales operation must tailor its strategy to each individual foreign country, and often to several different markets within that country. For example, Latin America's huge distances and undeveloped transportation both force companies to adopt a very different selling style to reach people living in the countryside than it uses to sell in the major conurbations.

Globalization does not mean homogeneity. The demand for Coca-Cola and Big Macs seems healthy everywhere they are available, but the range of disposable income is very wide across the world and the power to consume varies with it. Nor do all people want the same things or use them for the same purposes – British consumers, for example, have resisted the introduction of iced tea as a soft drink because many believe that tea should only be drunk hot, while in south-east Asia many local and foreign brands of iced tea are successful. Conversely the durian, a strong-smelling fruit (it has been described by Westerners as "like ice cream in a public lavatory") is so popular in south-east Asia that there is a wide variety of durian-flavored processed foods, including ice cream, sweets, and pastries, that are sold in well-known international chains – but it's unlikely that the durian flavor will catch on in Europe or North America.

Food, climate, and language are obvious basic differences, but they can still trip up the overconfident exporter. Political and economic differences can prove insurmountable; very few firms succeed in a foreign market without a subtle understanding of the realities of decision-making there. Coca-Cola chose to pull out of India for several years when a court demanded that it reveal its secret formula; when it returned it suffered widespread harassment from political agitators, who claimed – among other things – that the company was an agent of "American cultural imperialism." Competing soft-drink-makers are alleged to have had a hand in their problems.

Business-to-business sales in foreign countries may usually involve more sophisticated customers, but they do not necessarily make for easy sales. Price can be a crucial factor, and many Western firms make the mistake of assuming that the latest, most high-tech version of a product is necessarily the best for the customer. Ultra-modern equipment that works well in ideal conditions, near competent service engineers and in places where parts are less costly then labor, may be entirely inappropriate for locations with an abundance of cheap, unskilled workers, a harsh climate, and no spare parts. In such situations, exporters from countries such as Spain, Turkey, and Brazil often beat their competitors from northern Europe and the US, because they can supply cheaper equipment that is more reliable (or that can stand more abuse).

Across the developing world, from Peru to China, from Russia to Indonesia, companies are faced with petty corruption: underpaid officials, and indeed almost anyone in a position to do so, will ask for small ex gratia payments. What might seem outrageous at home is normal in many countries, so much so that even the draconian US anti-corruption legislation allows such payments as legitimate business expenses. High-level corruption, however, is more damaging. In the long term, bribery harms a firm because it can become an open-ended liability; a company may win a large order by paying a bribe, only to suffer what amounts to regular extortion in subsequent deals.

In spite of the difficulties, the overall climate is good for international sales growth. Many small- and medium-sized firms are successful internationally as are, by definition, the multinationals. With many markets becoming saturated in the industrialized world, going global is a major opportunity for growth. Given the potential rewards, it is clearly worthwhile to seek ways of penetrating foreign markets.

What are Global Sales?

» Who should sell overseas?
» Patience and sensitivity – a view from the field.
» Standardize or adapt?
» Country-of-origin effects.

"You'll never be the real thing if you're from out of town."
From the Coca-Cola Company 2000 Annual Report

For many multinationals, domestic selling has become a subset of global sales, and they have well-established and sophisticated systems of home-country nationals, third-country nationals, and local staff using strategies customized to individual territories.

WHO SHOULD SELL OVERSEAS?

Selling methods vary widely from country to country and must be designed carefully to fit local conditions; for example, cars are sold door to door in Japan, a method that is unlikely to catch on in Europe. Most firms use a combination of local and expatriate salespeople; sometimes expatriates can make a sale because they have higher prestige in the eyes of customers. The general trend, however, is towards increasing the proportion of local staff. Expatriates are expensive for their employers and hard to recruit; two major obstacles are the uprooting of an employee's family and the justifiable fear that working abroad will ruin career prospects at home. Today's expatriate salesperson often has a local spouse or some other strong connection with the host country that overrides the desire to return home. Some large companies make it clear that the route to the top must involve a period overseas, but in firms with poorly defined career paths a foreign posting can indeed be a ticket to a dead end.

International salespeople are now commonly frenetic travelers, making an endless series of trips to various countries and working closely with local staff before returning to headquarters. It's a role that requires maturity, wide international experience, and flexibility as well as mastery of selling skills. English is the language of international business, so multilingual ability is of secondary importance in many territories – in some countries, such as Turkey, being able to stutter a few mispronounced words can create enormous goodwill, while in others, such as France, it is perhaps better not to speak in the local language at all unless you are extremely fluent. Acquiring at least a conversational ability in the local language increases in importance for salespeople who are posted to the country for long periods – it's an act of politeness towards your hosts.

PATIENCE AND SENSITIVITY – A VIEW FROM THE FIELD

For smaller companies, entering foreign markets can be daunting. It's easy to lose sight of the basics of selling when you are confronted with a host of unfamiliar variables, but personal selling skills are often even more important than they are at home, especially in less developed countries. You are as much of an unknown quantity to your customers as they are to you, and the onus is on you to reassure them. Brad Buchholz, the vice-president of Laguna International, an SME based in California, emphasizes the importance of the personal touch, saying that one Japanese customer told him that the only reason why his group even considered working with Laguna was because of a personal meeting at a trade fair. In Africa, says Buchholz, he made the mistake of cold-calling to introduce his products; it was not until he started calling to introduce himself that sales began to happen. The introduction process gives the salesperson the opportunity to gauge the customer's perceived needs and tailor the selling strategy accordingly; an African customer complained to Buchholz of a small range of stock and competition from lower-priced Asian products. Buchholz tailored his subsequent presentation to these stated needs, going into great detail about how the firm could solve the problems by working closely with the customer. As Buchholz wryly points out, an essential factor in the presentation was that it was all true – the company could really deliver what was being promised.

In Africa, he found that the same objections were often repeated several times; taking this as a sign of interest, he offered more information enthusiastically. Closing was more difficult, and ultimatums were definitely to be avoided. Getting the initial sale took an inordinate amount of time and effort, and was not profitable – the rewards came later as increased trust resulted in repeat sales.[1]

STANDARDIZE OR ADAPT?

For more than 20 years, a debate has raged in large companies over whether it is better to standardize marketing methods internationally or to tailor methods to individual countries. According to one researcher, people's tastes diverge as they become better educated and richer[2] – which is, perhaps, surprising. Others have found that products need more modification in rural areas than in cities because of less availability and different media habits.[3] The case for standardization is essentially one of cost savings through economies of scale. Some argue that global customer groups are emerging that can be addressed in a homogeneous way. Kenichi Ohmae points out that North America, Europe, and Japan represent the lion's share of the market potential for most products, and that it is possible to standardize selling methods for many products across these regions.[4]

Academic researchers Cavusgil, Zou, and Naidu believe that managers can monitor over time their decision to standardize or adapt, and make adjustments to find the right combination. They argue that if competition in a given market is intense, adapting a product and its packaging, positioning, and promotion is likely to be essential.[5] Some firms may want standardization through a lack of experience in international markets, and are likely to fail, especially if they are selling consumer goods. Furthermore, different health, safety, and environmental regulations are likely to force companies to adapt their products or, at least, their packaging and labeling.

COUNTRY-OF-ORIGIN EFFECTS

Multinationals manufacture products all over the world, and in many markets they must indicate the country of origin, not just the brand name, on the packaging. Although such multinationals are generally vertically integrated and have excellent quality controls, there are worries that customers are prejudiced against products originating in certain countries and unfairly perceive them to be of poor quality. Much research has been done in the US to see which, if any, customer segments are influenced by country-of-origin labels.

A study by Victor Cordell of George Mason University found that:

» US consumers thought that shoes and watches from industrialized countries were of higher quality than those from less developed countries;

» industrialized countries were perceived to be product specialists – for example, consumers thought that Italy was the best for shoes, but poor for watches; and

» country-of-origin prejudice was more marked when the brand was unfamiliar, but still had an effect with well-known brands – for instance, Timex watches were slightly less popular when made in Pakistan than when made in Germany. Cordell concludes that it is safe for well-known brands to shift production to low-wage countries because the cost savings will far outweigh any small loss in sales.[6]

Consumers may also be averse to, say, buying a premium-priced Italian designer scarf if it is labeled "Made in China" even if they know that China produces fine silk; in this case, the objection is to the high price, not the quality.

Consumers in many developing countries tend to prefer foreign products from industrialized nations, and fads emerge everywhere; at the time of writing, China's consumers are demanding Western goods of all kinds, even when better substitutes are available.

Country-of-origin issues are of great concern to multinationals who analyze the trade-offs (for example, should Timex production be moved from Germany to Japan?) and design marketing strategies to mitigate negative country-of-origin effects. It seems that the stronger you make the brand, the less important the country-of-origin effects become, as is shown by Korea's success in winning a Western market share for its cars and electrical goods.

KEY LEARNING POINTS

» Expatriates versus local salespeople – as education and business experience improve around the world, the number of expatriates is reducing dramatically. Most firms with a local presence use a combination of foreign and local sales staff. Specialized international salespeople tend to make short-term visits to several countries when needed, working closely with local colleagues.

» Patience and the personal touch – in developing countries, where business life is less efficient and streamlined, customers place a high importance on personal trust. Developing this may take a lot of time, effort, and expense, and initial sales may be disappointing. Look for customers with the potential for a long-term relationship and don't expect instant profits. As one successful international seller puts it, "Don't think you can fly into somewhere like Russia, spend a week doing deals, and go home and forget about it. You'll be ripped off for sure."

» Standardization versus adaptation – it's expensive to adapt products to individual countries. Cost-saving through standardization is a powerful argument, but too often it is an excuse for rigidity; home-country managers may simply opt for standardization because modification just seems too much trouble. Adapting products is an ongoing process and may take time to generate the rewards, but large firms in many industries, from consumer goods to high-tech industrial machinery, are increasingly willing to take the trouble to do so as part of their quest for increased market share.

» Country of origin – there is ample evidence that customers give weight to country-of-manufacture information, irrespective of where the company itself is based. Customer perceptions of quality and value may be distorted by country-of-origin effects and have to be addressed carefully. Country-of-origin effects are weaker on well-known brands.

NOTES

1 Buchholz, B. (2002) "Practical exporting." *World Trade Magazine*, June 24. Available online at www.worldtrademag.com

2 Fisher, A.B. (1984) "The ad biz gloms onto 'global'." *Fortune*, November 12, pp. 77–80.

3 Hill, J.S. & Still, R.R. (1984) "Adapting products to LDC taste." *Harvard Business Review*, **62** (March–April), pp. 92–101.

4 Ohmae, K. (1985), *Triad Power: The coming shape of global competition*. The Free Press, New York.

5 Cavusgil, S.T., Zou, S., & Naidu, G.M. (1993) "Product and promotion adaptation in export ventures: an empirical investigation." *Journal of International Business Studies*, third quarter, pp. 479–502.

6 Cordell, V. (1992) "Effects of consumer preferences for foreign sourced products." *Journal of International Business Studies*, second quarter, pp. 251–69.

The Evolution of Global Sales

» From the nineteenth-century robber barons to the 1950s.
» Shipping.
» Europe and Japan recover.
» Busting a vitamin cartel.
» Timeline.

"How multitudinous are the devices by which industrialists have attempted to restrict international competition."

UK Board of Trade, 1944

Global sales have evolved with the development of international trade, which is discussed in detail in Chapter 3 of another book in the ExpressExec series, *Global Finance*. The evolution of sales techniques themselves is examined in Chapter 3 of *Sales Express*. In the present chapter we look at the development of global sales from a significant but less familiar angle, the phenomenon of price fixing by cartels. The evolution of global sales in this context is represented as a timeline in the box below.

TIMELINE

The following is a timeline showing the evolution of global sales, as influenced by the practice of price fixing.

» **1890**: The US introduces the Sherman Anti-Trust Act to break the power of the robber barons at home.
» **1929–1937**: An estimated 40% of world trade is controlled by international cartels.
» **1939**: Most international cartels collapse with the outbreak of World War II.
» **1945–1955**: In the decade following the end of World War II, US firms rush to export globally with little opposition. Pent-up demand, the collapse of business elsewhere, and US loans for reconstruction establish the US as the world's dominant exporter.
» **1960s**: Regenerated industries in Europe and Japan become international competitors with the US. Europe's governments act to limit US firms' power within their home markets. Developing countries try various methods of protecting their own markets from domination by foreign firms; there is a fashion for asset confiscation and currency blocking.
» **1970s**: The OPEC oil cartel dramatically forces up oil prices, sparking off a worldwide recession. Energy conservation

issues – once seen as part of the lunatic fringe of politics – become respectable for the first time.
» **1990s**: Governments, notably in Europe, begin to legislate against export cartels. Numerous prosecutions of cartels, many involving major firms, occur in the US and EU.

Most sales literature focuses on honing competitive skills in a relatively free marketplace, but what if there were little or no competition? Suppose your firm has a total monopoly on a much-desired product – making a sale would not take much effort or skill. This happy thought has occurred to business people throughout history, and many attempts have been made, with varying success, to maneuver firms into a position where they control a market either absolutely or in concert with a handful of competitors (a ''cartel''). Internationally, export cartels have often been supported by home governments on the grounds of national interest; the rationale has been that if a country's exporters occupy a powerful position in international markets, the nation can enrich itself by freeing export cartels from its domestic rules on fair competition.

From the point of view of an individual firm, export cartels are attractive so long as it is a member and the cartel is well run and sustainable (there is ample evidence that many, if not most, are not). Firms that are excluded from a cartel do not look upon them so kindly, while customers naturally object to being forced to pay more than is necessary.

FROM THE NINETEENTH-CENTURY ROBBER BARONS TO THE 1950S

Opportunities for cartels were dramatic in the nineteenth century, as Europe and America rapidly industrialized. New products and processes lent themselves to the concentration of market power. In the US, by the late nineteenth century the Rockefellers controlled oil refining, Carnegie controlled steel, Guggenheim controlled copper, du Pont controlled explosives, and James Duke dominated tobacco – all key commodities on which the country's economic development depended. The 1890 Sherman Anti-Trust Act was introduced to curb the power of these "robber barons" at home, but, like other industrializing nations, no such regulation was imposed on exports.

As competition between the developed countries increased, international cartels emerged as producers in different countries made agreements to divide up the world's markets between them, establish production quotas, and control prices. The heyday of the international cartel was during the interwar period; it is estimated that international cartels controlled some 40% of world trade between 1929 and 1937.

Some cartels are long-lived – De Beers controlled world diamond prices for more than a century – but they are difficult to sustain because of the incentive for cartel members to "cheat" on the agreement by secretly selling more than their quota or at a lower price. Other members follow, and the system quickly collapses. In industries with low entry barriers, cartels are virtually impossible to establish because new competitors can enter the market at any time. In concentrated industries with few producers, such as oil, it is much easier to create a cartel. The outbreak of World War II put an end to most of the international cartels, because member companies were on different sides and governments took control of industry.

SHIPPING

The international shipping industry has enjoyed close cooperation between competitors for more than 100 years. On the North Atlantic routes, steamship companies first tried to fix prices in the 1840s, but shipping cartels were already strongly established on the trade routes between Britain, India, and China.

Regular shipping conferences, a feature of the early twentieth century, fixed prices for cargo and passengers, and introduced the "pool," which divided the revenue pie between members and forced firms that exceeded their quotas to make cash payments to the ones who had lost out. Conference secretaries collected and analyzed the data to control the agreements. New competitors were vigorously opposed by price wars and also by making exclusive long-term deals with major exporters.

Governments have been amenable to the shipping industry's argument that the cartels help to stabilize the business, although it is probably spurious. In 1909, the UK's Royal Commission on Shipping Rings found that the conference system was necessary, as did the US Congress in 1914. At the end of World War I, the US insisted that conferences should not exclude any firm that wanted to join, however, and forced the cartels to register their agreements with a regulator.

After World War II, governments' attitudes began to change and efforts were made to limit the cartels' power; by 1974, the UN was pressing firms to allow shippers from less developed countries into the club. Container shipping, introduced in the 1960s, transformed the industry, making it more efficient and easier for new firms to compete. Since the 1980s, the US and Europe have increasingly restricted the cartels' power, but it is estimated that they still control more than two-thirds of the trade on the major routes around the world.

At the end of the war, the main focus of international business was on reconstruction; industrialized Europe and Japan were in ruins. Currencies were tied to the dollar, which alone was tied to gold, and there was a huge pent-up demand for goods of all kinds. Massive development aid, largely from the US, was supplied both to rebuild what had been lost and also to help foster capitalist economies in underdeveloped countries around the globe. Having built up a massive production capacity in the latter part of the war and now with a labor force enlarged by returning servicemen, the US was in a position to supply many of the goods that were so desperately needed. In 1948, the General Agreement on Tariffs and Trade (GATT) was established to try to lower trade barriers around the world gradually – since 1930, international trade had been severely limited by protectionist policies.

For the next 10 years, growth was rapid and global living standards generally rose. Outside the communist bloc, US firms dominated most markets as exporters, and soon began to establish production bases abroad to supply local demand. According to Richard D. Robinson, Professor of International Management at the Alfred P. Sloan School of Management, there was little political interference during this period. Host countries were eager for American dollars and goods, and international business was left to exporters and their customers across the globe.[1]

By the mid-1950s, Europe and Japan had recovered to the point where they wanted to export for themselves. Dollar-priced goods became relatively more expensive, and US firms suddenly faced competition from abroad. Large US exporters began to transform into multinational concerns with integrated global marketing and production systems. Elsewhere, governments began to take notice of business and to look for ways of making their own economies stronger – new strains of nationalism and complaints about "neo-colonialism" led to increased regulation of business by many host countries during a period of rapid growth. How and what you sold began to depend as much upon the host country's attitude towards your own as it did upon actual demand, while socialist policies in Western Europe imposed heavy constraints on domestic firms, many of which were, in any case, government-owned.

Since the nineteenth century, the US had been at the forefront of innovation in selling, largely because of its vast and relatively homogeneous internal market. In 1841, the first advertising agency was established in Philadelphia. In 1856, the first full-page advertisement appeared in a newspaper. Branded consumer goods such as Coca-Cola and Singer sewing machines were aggressively marketed from the late 1800s, while Ford's invention of the production line made it possible for there to be 3.5 million cars on US roads by 1916. By the 1950s, mass-marketing techniques that had been perfected in the US were being applied around the world by American, European, and, increasingly, Japanese firms.

EUROPE AND JAPAN RECOVER

In the 1960s, resistance to US exporters became intense. European governments began to restrict US investment within their countries and impose regulations to protect their own industries. The French writer J.J. Servan-Schreiber, in his 1968 book *The American Challenge*, warned darkly that "fifteen years from now it is quite possible that the world's third greatest industrial power, just after the United States and Russia, will not be Europe but American industry in Europe."[2] In other parts of the world, opposition was more dramatic. Many developing countries, particularly in Latin America, seized the assets of foreign companies with little or no compensation, or froze their cash so it could not be taken home.

The oil crises of the early 1970s were a watershed in the world economy. The Organization of Petroleum-Exporting Countries (OPEC), a producers' cartel that supplied 67% of the industrialized world's oil, raised prices from $10 a barrel to $50 a barrel, setting off a worldwide recession. It was a sharp wake-up call; since then, strenuous efforts have been made to consume energy more efficiently and OPEC's power has weakened. Recently, however, dramatic industrial development in countries such as China has put enormous pressure on the world's energy resources. During the 1990s, the world's dependence on OPEC oil began to return to pre-1970s' levels, and there is general recognition that close international cooperation is needed to prevent a serious collapse of global trade in the future.

During the 1990s, one feature of the globalization trend has been that national governments are more inclined to act against export cartels on free trade grounds – freer trade means more productivity and wealth for everyone, so the theory goes, and this implies that countries should not act selfishly by supporting export cartels that benefit their own firms while protesting against others that do not. Cartel arrangements tend to be secretive, but a flurry of court cases has revealed evidence of collusion in a very wide range of industries.

The US and the EU have been prominent in prosecuting cartels, whose members have included many major international companies from their own countries and also from Japan and South Korea. Major firms are trying hard to gain access to closed markets by making complaints under new anti-trust legislation; Kodak, for instance, complains that it is blocked from selling its products in Japan by a local cartel, while the European aircraft-maker Airbus Industrie is accused of colluding with local suppliers to prevent non-EU suppliers from selling spare parts to airlines using Airbus planes. Elsewhere, the main Colombian beer brewer is alleged to have market-sharing deals with its competitors at home and in neighbouring countries, while the Mexican government is said to be involved in preventing entrants into its domestic market for high-fructose corn syrup (used as a sweetener in processed food). The EU and the US have successfully prosecuted cartels including companies from all over the world, such as Malaysia (shipping), Brazil (aluminum phosphide), Israel (bromine), Canada (plastic dinnerware), Finland (steel heating pipes), South Africa (newsprint), and India (aluminum phosphide).

The anti-trust issue is heated, particularly in the US. Major firms claim to have been "victimized" by their suppliers' cartels, yet are often involved in collusion with their own competitors. Civil servants characterize cartel activity as criminal and urge the EU to imprison the executives involved. Developing countries pay lip service to free trade ideals, yet often encourage local firms to resist foreign entrants to their markets. Everywhere there are mixed messages, but one thing is clear – no foreign sales strategy is complete unless it takes into account the existing arrangements for collusion within that market.

BUSTING A VITAMIN CARTEL

In 1999 the Swiss pharmaceutical giant F. Hoffmann-La Roche Ltd pleaded guilty in a US court to charges that it had organized a "worldwide conspiracy" to fix prices and apportion market shares in the worldwide vitamin business. Roche paid a fine of $500mn, while another cartel member, the German company BASF, paid $225mn. The cartel had been uncovered by means of information from the French firm Rhone-Poulenc, which had also been involved, but had been given protection from prosecution.

The cartel arrangement, which had run from 1990 to 1999, involved vitamins used as nutritional supplements or to enrich human food and animal feed, such as vitamins A, B_2, and C, and betacarotene. Vitamin "premixes," sold to companies such as Kellogg's, were a major part of the business. The cartel had rigged bids for contracts to customers, raised prices on vitamins, and carefully divided market shares and sales volume between its members.

Swiss national Dr Kuno Sommer, the director of Worldwide Marketing, Hoffmann-La Roche Vitamins and Fine Chemicals Division, pleaded guilty to being involved in the cartel and lying to US investigators. He was fined $100,000 and sentenced to four months in prison.

KEY LEARNING POINTS

» In concentrated industries where there are few players, there is a strong incentive to cooperate with the competition by dividing up market share and setting high prices.

» Historically, industrialized countries supported export cartels that benefited their own companies, while often forbidding similar practices at home.

» Rapid industrialization in the nineteenth century allowed commercial power to be concentrated in very few hands, at least in the short to medium term. By the early twentieth century, there were many international cartel agreements between producers in the industrialized world (notably the US, the UK, Germany, and France).

» Cartels often fail because of the temptation for members to "cheat" on agreements. Due to the secretive nature of cartels, there is controversy over the duration and failure rates.

» One of the most successful cartels is in the shipping industry, where major lines have openly colluded on prices and excluded competitors for well over a century.

» In line with the free trade philosophy, many governments today have legislation against cartels. During the 1990s there have been numerous prosecutions, and a window has been opened on these discreet arrangements.

» When entering a new foreign market, it is clearly vital to assess whether any collusive arrangements exist and to consider how best to meet this challenge.

NOTES

1 Robinson, R.D. (1987) "Some new competitive factors in international marketing." *Advances in International Marketing*, **1**, pp. 1–20.

2 Servan-Schreiber, J.J. (1968) *The American Challenge* (trans. R. Steel). Hamish Hamilton, London.

The E-Dimension

» The consumer markets.
» Cannibalization.
» Travel.
» Best practice? – Boo.com

"If you build it, he will come."

Kevin Costner in the 1989 movie Field of Dreams

Despite the dot.com bust, the hype about e-commerce continues. A multitude of firms wish to market their e-commerce solutions at you, and a host of consultants, investment banks, and trade journals eagerly continue to predict extraordinary international growth. But what's the truth? What sells on the Internet, and is it profitable?

THE CONSUMER MARKETS

Around the world, the following product types are the top sellers online:

» books;
» music/CDs;
» electronics/electrical goods;
» holidays/travel; and
» PC hardware and software.

Internet penetration continues to deepen around the world, but being an Internet user is not the same as being an Internet shopper; globally, an average 15% of Internet users actually made purchases online in 2001–2. In the US one in three Internet users makes purchases, and South Korea is not far behind. Germany's conversion rate is 26%, Norway's is 25%, and the UK's is 23%. Curiously, the Internet's value as a sales aid, providing information for purchases made in the "real" world, is equivalent to online purchases as a percentage of Internet users – an average 15% globally. These figures did not change from the previous year.[1]

Growth forecasts continue to be inaccurate, even after the burst of the dot.com investment bubble, but nevertheless online consumer sales are already worth tens of billions of dollars in the US alone. According to the online retailers' association Shop.org, only 56% of online retailers in the US made a profit in 2001, with online catalogue companies doing best at an average 6% operating profit. Shop.org predicts that US e-tailers will break even overall in 2002.

An average 6% profit? Only half the e-tailers make a profit in the most Internet-savvy country in the world? This is hardly a fulfillment of the heady promises made in the boom days of the late 1990s. Nevertheless, it is clear that it is possible to sell in quantity online to consumers and even sometimes to make money doing it, if the product is right.

Books are still the biggest-selling product line, dominated by Amazon. During 2000, Amazon was the top online retail site in every country in Western Europe in terms of visits. But the company, the quintessential online retailer, failed to make a profit in almost six years after its start-up in 1995. Finally, in the last quarter of 2001, it claimed a $5mn profit (30% of sales were non-US), before slipping back into the red in 2002. With $2.2bn in debt, Amazon has been under pressure to cut costs, particularly in stock management – the warehouses it built are now seen as a costly mistake. Ventures into other product lines have been generally unsuccessful, and its core business remains books, music, and CDs. Customers appreciate the convenience of shopping at Amazon; in many countries, ordering a foreign book from a bookstore can mean a wait of three months or more. Timely delivery and a comprehensive online catalogue are a powerful inducement to buy in an industry where, worldwide, consumers outside major cities have immense difficulty in obtaining the goods that they want. From the point of view of sales alone, Amazon has got its formula right with its core product lines – but will it ever make real money with them?

IT goods seem to be more promising. PC manufacturer Dell starting selling computers online in 1996 and by 2001 it had become the market leader in PCs worldwide, with nearly 50% of its sales made via the Internet. According to Scott Eckert, director of Dell Online, the company's online success is due to a good understanding of their customers' needs: "Customers value quick and easy access to products. They enjoy shopping at their leisure. And they want information   lots of information. The Web gives them all of that ... We create clear entry points for people from different sectors: business, home office, education. We have nearly 40 country-specific versions of the sites, and each one uses the appropriate language and currency."

Eckert reports that Web customers visit the Dell site many times before they buy, saving their bespoke configurations on-site for up to two weeks while they compare them with competitors' products. Interestingly, he claims that customers "talk themselves into" buying more expensive systems without the prompting of a salesperson. Eckert believes that making the Website user-friendly is a key to sales – an "Order Status" feature, for example, tells customers what stage their order has reached in the assembly/delivery process.[2]

CANNIBALIZATION

Across the world, many manufacturers and intermediaries worry that the Internet will destroy value by "cannibalizing" business already going through other channels. Middlemen are worried that they will be cut out of the equation by direct sales online. Manufacturers in turn fear that direct selling online will cause their existing distributors to give less support to their products or even switch to their competitors. In 1999, for example, jeans-maker Levi Strauss pulled its online Website because of objections from its intermediaries. A 1998 article in the *Harvard Business Review* warned that "Established businesses that over decades have carefully built brands and physical distribution relationships risk damaging all they have created when they pursue commerce in cyberspace,"[3] while *Fortune* magazine called it "survival by suicide."[4]

Why should Internet sales "steal" from other sales channels? There are three main arguments.

1 Easier access, more information, and other benefits may encourage existing customers to switch to buying online.
2 Online customers find it much easier to compare prices.
3 Online buying may prevent impulse purchases.

One counter-argument is that Websites may actually increase offline sales because of the easier access to information – the customer may investigate the product online before purchasing at a store. Another point is that while the Internet may disrupt sales channels in the short term, the real question is whether it permanently cannibalizes.

The newspaper industry is particularly affected by the Internet, which can deliver news more quickly and allows the customer search facilities. Newspapers are a mature business where competition is seen as a zero-sum game. Online editions, which are frequently free, may potentially cannibalize existing newspaper readers, forcing down circulation and consequently reducing advertising revenues.

A study of 85 newspapers with online editions in Holland and the UK attempted to discover whether cannibalization fears were justified and found that only a few suffered a significant drop in income from sales and advertising.[5] The reasons for this may be that online newspaper readers tend to be young, educated, and Internet-savvy – quite different from the typical newspaper reader – and online advertisers are generally not print advertisers. Print advertisers are typically department stores and retail chains, while online advertisers tend to be IT-related.

The researchers point out that keeping the online edition qualitatively different from the print edition helps to prevent cannibalization, and found that the few newspapers in the study that did suffer revenue losses tended to have online editions that were close copies of the hard-copy paper.

Sony raised cannibalization fears in its dealer network recently when it launched a Website in Japan to sell VAIO personal computers and peripherals directly to consumers. Like Dell, Sony offers customers the chance to customize their PCs by choosing the memory size, peripherals, and software. The company hopes to achieve sales of $95.2mn (a remarkably precise figure) in its first year online.

Sony says it will soon add other products to its online range – including digital cameras, music players, and televisions – and provide frequent customers with free Internet access. The company's president Nobuyuki Ideo has stated that he wants to eventually create an "e-empire", selling up to 40% of its products online. The VAIO computers it offers through its Website, however, will not be sold through retail outlets.

TRAVEL

Travel lends itself well to online selling because of the lack of transparency in ticket prices and availability offline. Growth has been strong; in 1999, online travel sales were $6.9bn, rising to $20bn in 2001 despite the damage to the industry caused by the September 11 attacks. According to Jupiter Research, 80% of online travel bookings in 2000 were for leisure and personal trips,[6] while a survey by PhoCusWright found that 60% of customers thought that price was the most important factor when buying.

PhoCusWright's CEO, Philip Wolf, says, "Online travel is still the e-commerce killer app, despite a very battered market."[7]

BEST PRACTICE? – BOO.COM

Dell makes money, unlike Boo.com, a London-based global fashion retailer that went spectacularly bankrupt in 2000.[8]

Boo was founded by two achingly hip young Swedes, Ernst Malmsten and Kajsa Leander (a former model), who had a track record of minor entrepreneurial success, including starting an online bookstore in Sweden named bokus. They sold bokus for several million in March 1998 to KF, a Swedish conglomerate, less than a year after launching the site.

Flushed with their success, Malmsten and Leander decided to set up an online fashion retailer aimed at young, sophisticated Europeans. The goal was to create a Europe-wide brand that also had global appeal. Unlike books and CDs, designer clothes are not discounted, so margins can be kept relatively high.

The main challenge was how to persuade customers to buy clothes that they could not try on. The partners decided to "create the first fully-branded shopping experience on the Net" using advanced 3D imaging that enabled customers to spin clothing images around on screen and "dress" an online mannequin with the items they selected. The virtual mannequin, "Miss Boo," also acted as a sales assistant, complete with slick, cool dialogue.

Boo's prototype Website wowed investors, especially those who were well established in the fashion industry. Benetton and Louis Vuitton Moet Hennessy invested, and the prestigious merchant bank J P Morgan agreed to nurse the start-up through to the hoped-for IPO.

The prestige of the investors and the impressive Website brought in major suppliers, and Boo was announced in a blaze of free publicity in May 1999. Everyone seemed to love Boo's glamorous "Eurobrat" image and its plans to operate the site in multiple language versions. An initial "holding page" on the Internet asking customers to register received tens of thousands of hits each day. Within three months 230,000 people had registered.

Difficulties in constructing the technically ambitious site caused delays, and it was not until October that Boo was able to run a "soft launch," offering password access to the site for "family and friends" of the company. Customers were offered heavily discounted goods in return for completing a detailed marketing questionnaire.

The following month saw the full launch, generating an enthusiastic response from the media. The *New York Post*, for example, called Boo "the hottest looking e-tailing site ever," but Mac users complained of difficulties in accessing the site.

Boo received 228,000 visits in the first week, resulting in 609 orders worth a total of $64,000. Within six weeks, they had sold goods worth $350,000 (an average order value of $115) and the view-to-order conversion rate had doubled. By the end of the first trading quarter, net revenues had reached $0.7mn. By the end of February 2000, net revenues had doubled.

Meanwhile, big league investors' enthusiasm for the Internet had waned, and the company was rapidly running out of cash. Despite growing sales, repeat custom, and speedy delivery, Boo was in serious trouble as it became clear that the stock markets were unlikely to welcome yet another Internet offering. Investors who had been hoping for an easy exit were now faced with the prospect of supporting the firm for years, and began to get cold feet.

An email promotion at Easter offering a discount of $30 on future purchases provoked a deluge of orders, at one point jamming the Website. Gross sales in the first two weeks of May were $500,000, 40% of which were repeat customers. Investors, however, were unwilling to advance any more money, and the company went into liquidation.

Boo may have flopped as a company, but as an online sales organization it had flair. Identifying the large market of affluent young Europeans who wish to wear designer clothes that they cannot buy except by traveling to a major city, often in another country, the firm successfully caught their interest and quickly achieved substantial sales. Although Boo's Website was criticized as being "too advanced," it achieved its objective of being perceived by its market as attractive and "cool"; technical problems were solved quickly, and mass emailing to registered visitors was effective. Access to the Website in the customer's own language was a major element in creating a positive image – at the time, many people, in Europe and elsewhere, were complaining that too much of the content of the Web was intended only for Americans. Many Europeans did not have credit cards and were uncomfortable about using them on the Web, so Boo's positive image was vital in winning customer confidence.

Notwithstanding the illusion of the single market, it was still not easy to move goods around Europe. Boo packed its goods in Cologne, Germany, but had to attach a French postal service label to the box for customers in France. Any returns would go to a collection point before being shipped back to Germany. Portugal refused to accept bar codes on imported packages, and identification codes had to be specially written. The firm coped with the bureaucratic challenges and achieved a 96% on time delivery rate. Within 18 months, Boo had created an internationally known brand using $130mn of their investors' money – a feat that has taken other firms decades to achieve.

KEY LEARNING POINTS

The rapid pace of change in the business-to-consumer online markets will doubtless throw up new selling techniques and insights as the Internet continues to develop and mutate, but there are already some signs of transferable rules.

- Translate your Website. Consumers prefer to be sold to in their own language, even if they speak English. Faced with a choice between competing sites, they are likely to prefer the one that has made the effort to bridge the language gap.
- Online sales work best when they offer customers benefits that cannot be obtained offline. Low price is a benefit, but so is giving access to goods that people cannot buy locally.

» So far, the range of products that sell well online is quite limited. Most of them (books, music, air tickets) are businesses where the customer wants a specific item out of a staggeringly wide range – "I don't want just any book, I want the latest Elmore Leonard" or "I don't want just any CD, I want the George Michael Album."

» The medium is the message. Techies use the Internet heavily for their work, and it comes naturally to them to make purchases online.

» Reliable, speedy delivery is essential. Consumers are reluctant to wait. If they must wait, they are consoled by being able to check the progress of the delivery online. Parcel carrier DHL offers customers the facility to follow the movement of a package across the globe using the waybill code.

» Have a range of payment options. Credit cards are still not widely available in many countries, and many consumers are reluctant to use them online for fear of fraud. Offer the credit card payment facility as well as other payment methods, and back up the order system with a call center to field enquiries.

» Use the Web to boost offline sales by providing full product information online.

» Publicize the Website through the traditional media channels. With the possible exception of specialized IT products, customers will not go out of their way to find your obscure Website unless they know about it already. Don't rely on search engines to bring visitors to your site.

» Tailor foreign-language versions of the Website to the culture and conditions of the country concerned. Everything, from colors and images to the description of the product, should be examined carefully for appropriateness.

» Make a profit! Yahoo, eBay, and Dell have been profitable for years. With capital less freely available, the "if you build it, they will come" philosophy of the Internet boom is looking increasingly thin.

NOTES

1 Taylor Nelson Sofres (2002) *The TNS Interactive - Global eCommerce Report 2002*. Available online at www.tnsofres.com/ger2002/home.cfm

2 Chadderdon, L. (1998) "How Dell sells on the Web." *Fast Company*, September.

3 Ghosh, S. (1998) "Making business sense of the Internet." *Harvard Business Review*, **76**:2, pp. 126-35.

4 Useem, J. (1999) "Internet defense strategy: cannibalize yourself." *Fortune*, September 6, pp. 121-34.

5 Deleersnyder, B., Geyskens, I., Gielens, K., & Dekimpe, M.G. (2001) "How cannibalistic is the internet channel?" Working paper, Penn State University, eBusiness Research Center.

6 Jupiter's proprietary research quoted in "From 'fantastic' to 'solid growth': online travel still looks good," February 18, (2000). Available online at www.cendant.com

7 PhoCusWright (2001) "Sixteen travel industry luminaries to address delegates in Miami." Press release, October 5.

8 Malmsten, E., Portanger, E., & Drazin, C. (2001), *Boo hoo: A dot.com story from concept to catastrophe*. Random House Business, London.

The Global Dimension

» Quality.
» Packaging and labeling.
» The metric system.
» ISO 9000.
» Global demand.
» Best practice varies across the globe.

"Bite the wax tadpole."
The literal meaning of Coca-Cola's first attempt at
transliterating its name into Chinese in the 1920s

Going global does not usually mean selling more of exactly the same products that you sell at home. More often than not, products and selling methods have to be adapted to individual local markets, both because of customers' demands and because of different standards of measurement and product regulations. The scope for costly errors is enormous. In this chapter, we will look at some commonly encountered problems and how they can be solved.

QUALITY

"Quality" does not have to mean "best quality," even when it is clear what "best quality" should be. In the early days of jet travel, for instance, the US suffered from high labor costs while Britain had high fuel costs, and their planes reflected this – US jets were designed for easy engine access to make repair and servicing easier, while British jets had an aerodynamic design that reduced fuel consumption. Both were high-quality products, but intended for different market conditions. Today, less developed countries often do not require the latest state-of-the-art product, for good reasons. Labor costs are lower at home, so the labor-saving features of products may not be worth paying for. If workers are unskilled or there is no mass-scale production, modern industrial machines may be less desirable than a dependable, labor-intensive 1950s' model.

The key to success in less developed markets is in offering a product that matches the customer's needs as closely as possible. Price is usually a key factor, and customers are likely to prefer the product that fits their price and quality requirements over a high-quality/high-priced competitor.

PACKAGING AND LABELING

Packaging and labeling rules can be the exporter's nightmare. Consumer lobby groups, environmentalism, protectionism, and politics all contribute to the morass of conflicting regulations across the globe. Food and medicine are particularly closely controlled everywhere because of the potential dangers to consumers, but few, if any, products can escape the regulatory net entirely.

Historical and cultural factors can lead to surprises, as illustrated below.

» It is illegal in Germany to distribute "unannotated hate literature" such as Hitler's autobiography, *Mein Kampf*. In 1999, German publishing giant Bertelsmann had to withdraw the book from the French and English versions of its online bookstore, because Germans are able to order goods from these Web pages. In the same year, the Simon Wiesenthal Center in Los Angeles complained to the German Justice Ministry that Barnes & Noble and Amazon.com were violating German law by selling hate literature to German customers.

» Genetically modified food and animals that have eaten it are not considered halal in many Muslim countries and are therefore banned.

» In 2000, a $17bn trade deal between the EU and South Africa ran into trouble because of complaints that South Africa was producing alcoholic drinks with names that are protected in the EU, such as "grappa" and "ouzo." South Africa produces small quantities of these drinks and accused some European countries of using the issue to slow down the whole treaty, which is intended to remove tariff barriers between the regions almost completely over the next decade.

» Many countries require the translation of essential labeling information into the local language, but not everyone goes as far as Mexico, which specifies that the Spanish-language information on a label must be "at least the same size and typographical proportion and in a manner which is equally ostensible" as information in another language, and that it "must appear in a similar or equivalent location with the same or similar colors and designs, for both the print and the background."[1]

» In the US, enzymes used in food processing that are "cooked out" before they reach the consumer – such as dough conditioners and artificial leaveners – do not have to appear on product labels. In Canada, however, they must be listed.

THE METRIC SYSTEM

The US government feels that the country suffers a competitive disadvantage in exports because so many firms resist using the metric system, as do US consumers. The US has never had a single official system of weights and measures, and has not prohibited the use of traditional systems in many key areas, such as education, construction, and retailing. While metric lobbyists in the US point to this absurdity by claiming that only the US, Myanmar, and Liberia are non-metric, this is not strictly true – the US has simply not adopted the metric system with any firmness.

This is bad for business and science, and legislators have tried to do something about it. The 1988 Omnibus Trade and Competitiveness Act states that "the metric system of measurement is the preferred system of weights and measures for United States trade and commerce," and forces all government agencies to use metric measurements in almost all of their activities, with the notable exception of certain documents aimed at consumers.

The US no longer dominates world trade to the overwhelming extent that it did in the postwar era, and there is a general recognition that foreign markets are keen for the US to convert to what is now the global standard. The huge inefficiencies of operating two systems are increasing, and the government is faced with the difficult challenge of persuading its citizens to endure the short-term hardship of conversion.

THE LOSS OF THE MARS CLIMATE ORBITER

In 1999 the *Mars Climate Orbiter*, an unmanned spacecraft, dived into Mars's atmosphere and disappeared, causing a $125mn loss to NASA. The reason was quickly identified and proved to be embarrassing; an engineering team at Lockheed Martin had used English units of measurement that other teams interpreted as metric, leading to the navigation error that sent the *Orbiter* to its doom.

According to NASA's Tom Gavin, "This is an end-to-end process problem ... a single error like this should not have caused the loss of *Climate Orbiter*. Something went wrong in our system processes in checks and balances that we have that should have caught this and fixed it."

Incredibly, NASA still allows imperial measures to be used in certain circumstances. After the Omnibus Trade and Competitiveness Act was passed in 1988, NASA made efforts to convert to the metric system and developed specifications for metric parts to be produced by manufacturers. Meanwhile, certain large NASA project teams decided to continue to use the imperial system, including the Space Station Program and the Aeronautics and Research Technology Program, which receive about 25% of NASA's total funding. Other programs use "hard" metric systems (quoting measures principally as metric), "soft" metric systems (quoting imperial measures with the metric equivalent following), and "hybrid" systems (where both metric and imperial units are allowed, as with the *Orbiter*).

What's the problem?

NASA staff reported the following reasons for retaining the imperial system.

» Many manufacturers do not use the metric system, so parts must be specially made, causing delays and increased cost. Standard aeronautical parts are made using the imperial system in the US, and NASA's buying power is not great enough to force many manufacturers to convert.

» "Hybrid" programs using both systems of measurement force double calculation, leading to errors and what is perceived by many to be a waste of time.

» Engineers felt that while they had an "intuitive" grasp of the outcomes of calculations and the use of hardware expressed in imperial units, they were working in the dark when using metric units. Older engineers were particular resistant to conversion.

ISO 9000

Set up in 1946, the International Organization for Standardization (ISO) promotes the use of ISO 9000, a series of international industrial standards intended to provide a system of quality assurance.

Although almost always voluntary, ISO 9000 is strongly pushed by certain regulators, notably the EU, whose EU Product Liability Directive makes manufacturers liable, regardless of fault or negligence, for personal injury resulting from product failure due to a faulty component. A manufacturing firm exporting to EU countries, therefore, should at least consider obtaining ISO certification.

The ISO system is often criticized as bureaucratic and expensive, yet it is not solely driven by civil servants. Global trade often means doing business with strangers, and the ISO provides a weak form of independent guarantee to the customer that the supplier will deliver acceptable goods.

Particularly within the EU, where firms risk heavy sanctions if they sell defective products, many business buyers insist that their suppliers have ISO certification, while others will give preference to an ISO holder over an uncertified competitor. Firms selling products using components manufactured in China, for example, almost certainly need ISO to sell in the EU.

ISO is catching on elsewhere too; the Japanese government insists on ISO for its construction purchases and the standard is seen as increasingly important in global high-tech hardware manufacturing worldwide. To date, about 400,000 firms around the world have registered for ISO.

The standards are not product-specific, but relate to generic processes. The purpose is to establish that a company has an adequate system of quality control, not to guarantee that it makes "quality" products. To apply, a firm must approach an authorized certifying body (which is independent of the ISO organization) and ask for an assessment of its key business processes. This audit covers a host of detailed matters, from filing methods to the percentage of late deliveries, and asks for evidence of customer satisfaction. The assessor assists the company in writing a comprehensive manual of its quality processes, which is available for inspection by customers. Once the company conforms to the assessor's requirements, it receives certification and undergoes periodical reviews and recertification thereafter. Alternatively, it can choose to show "compliance" with ISO rather than go through the certification process.

These procedures have engendered complaints about the assessors. Some assessors are alleged to be abusing their power, using idiosyncratic or overly narrow interpretations of the ISO guidelines. Forthcoming are newer versions of the ISO that are intended to streamline the auditing process and prevent it becoming an arbitrary checklist, but clearly the success of the audit depends largely upon the caliber of the auditors.

Although ISO is intended for companies of all sizes, large firms may find it easier to cope with ISO compliance because they already have quality-control systems in place. Cutting-edge manufacturers such as Motorola have commented that their existing quality systems are far superior to the ISO requirements. Dan Whelan, manager of quality systems standards at Ford, says, "We supplemented the standard and interpreted it to fit our business. ISO is out there as a mechanism. We recognized that if we didn't improve the ISO 9000 and make it value-added, the whole thing would collapse, and we didn't want that." The large car-makers are attempting to work within the existing ISO system, but can "walk away from ISO tomorrow" if things don't work out, according to Whelan.[2]

ISO and sales

So how does ISO affect salespeople? Much depends upon the level of commitment at the top; if the board sees ISO as an unwelcome annoyance, it is unlikely that the sales department will take it seriously. Similarly, sales managers who are not committed to the process are unlikely to inspire ISO enthusiasm in the sales force.

One potential source of conflict is in how sales performance is measured. If a sales team is solely focused on achieving sales targets, ISO compliance may be regarded as getting in the way of real work. Sales teams may regard pronouncements on customer relations by outsiders as an incursion into their territory – salespeople may, with some justification, feel that they are far more concerned with customer satisfaction on a daily basis than the desk-bound administrators who are imposing ISO on them from above.

ISO is not for every firm. If, however, there are clear and demonstrable benefits to be had from certification, such as entry into a

European market, it is possible to tie quality standards to sales results and integrate them into the process of sales management.

GLOBAL DEMAND

Surprisingly, industrial markets are much more volatile than consumer markets, which makes global diversification an important strategy for producers. A major factor in this volatility is purchasers' rapidity of response to change. Computer manufacturers, for instance, monitor the demand for PCs – a slight drop in consumer demand can result in all major purchasers reducing their orders for components within a short period, creating a sudden knock-on effect up the supply chain. The pressures for efficiency in stock control and reducing prices make industrial purchasers far more sensitive to change than their consumer counterparts.

Demand that depends on behavior in another market is known as derived demand – for example, if consumers move to a new kind of holiday, the demand for aircraft will be affected.

MISJUDGING GLOBAL DEMAND – THE IRIDIUM STORY

In the early 1990s, mobile telephony had not yet taken off. High-tech giant Motorola and other partners began planning a fantastically ambitious scheme to launch a large number of satellites that would enable cellphones to work anywhere in the world. The idea was that senior executives and government officials would be happy to pay hefty fees to use the service, which was to be offered by a new company, Iridium.

Iridium special phones were bulky, only worked if they were in the line of sight of a satellite (so could not often be used indoors), had heavy power needs, and cost some $3000 each. With no other competitors, this was not seen as a problem, as the firm drew up confident plans to capture the lucrative business travel market. Iridium phones were to be sold around the world to an estimated 50,000 customers by 2000.

While Iridium struggled with the enormous technical challenges of launching 66 low-orbiting satellites, terrestrial mobile phone systems began to grow rapidly. Iridium's triumph in launching the system in late 1998 gave way to despair as it became plain that most business travelers had no need for the product – they were signing up to cheaper, more effective land-based systems that already gave good coverage of the world's major cities. Iridium would have to look for more specialized phone users who were traveling in remote areas, such as geologists and military personnel, but this would be a tiny market (only some 2% of the value of the global mobile phone business).

By 2000, Iridium was out of business, owing billions, having seen its intended market evaporate. "What they didn't do was to focus on, analyze and pay attention to the market they could serve," commented space industry consultant Carissa Christensen.[3]

BEST PRACTICE VARIES ACROSS THE GLOBE

Globalization? – the extraordinary diversity of distribution structures worldwide

In the developed countries we are used to mass consumption, heavy competition, and a buyer's market where the customer is king. Distribution channels are intricate and sophisticated, with a great variety of intermediaries. Japan's distribution structure has the most complexity of all (see below) but in other parts of the world, the situation is very different. Many less developed countries still have an import-oriented system, where there is a limited supply of goods controlled by a small number of importers principally serving an elite market of expatriates and affluent locals. Demand exceeds supply, and this seller's market forces Western exporters to adopt very different selling methods from what they are familiar with at home. The powerful importers/wholesalers tend to dominate the system, focusing on the most profitable segments – there are no fully integrated countrywide distribution channels.

The general trend across the world is to evolve away from the import-oriented system towards the mass-market model we know in the West – in some respects, this could almost be a definition of economic development – but since countries vary so widely in terms of land mass, population, climate, and political stability, there is little prospect of developing a truly homogeneous globalized distribution structure. Outside the developed West, one factor stands out – it is generally necessary to use local agents or distributors if one is to have any chance of success in foreign markets.

To grasp the range of distribution systems across the world, it is worth examining a contrasting selection in more detail.

Congo

The Congo's economy is in ruins, and doing business there necessitates converting payments into foreign currency as quickly as possible. Smuggling is rife, and most firms use informal arrangements to avoid the local banking system.

Belgian, Lebanese, and east Asian firms dominate, focusing principally on selling to the government and the expatriate community in the main cities. With few roads, expensive air transport, and inefficient barge traffic, prices outside the main centers vary greatly according to access.

Peru

Almost a third of Peru's population lives in Lima, so firms concentrate most of their selling efforts there, with a limited presence in provincial towns via sales agents. A very price-sensitive market, Peru buys heavily from low-cost manufacturers in countries such as Taiwan and South Korea, and high-quality Western goods are a hard sell, except for capital purchases where quality is perceived as essential. Radio and newspapers are the main ways of advertising, but television is increasing its penetration. Import tariffs are relatively low, averaging around 9%, and distributors' mark-ups range from 12% to 25%.

Turkey

Turkey has a large population (over 65 million) but most foreign products are sold through local agents or distributors due to bureaucratic complexities, the language barrier, and the vital importance of personal relationships. Agents are responsive to support, and welcome the opportunity to visit the exporter's country for annual sales meetings. Many exporters periodically visit important existing and potential customers with their local agent. There are some 70 trade shows annually in Turkey, and they are seen as an effective way of developing sales.

Turkish companies tend to lack capital, and some foreign firms find that flexible financing arrangements that reduce upfront cash payments are an important sales inducement.

Vietnam

Foreign firms must use local importers by law unless they have a local manufacturing subsidiary, in which case they are sometimes allowed to sell goods domestically. Vietnam's distribution network is split between the south, the north and the central areas of the country and is highly fragmented with a large number of middlemen. The booming economy has brought rapid change in some areas, with convenience stores and large shopping malls appearing, such as the Saigon Superbowl in Ho Chi Minh City, and French developer CORA's hypermarket project near Hanoi. Consumerism is on the rise and people, especially in the south, are remarkably knowledgeable about international brands. Ho Chi Minh City (formerly Saigon), is regarded as the primary center for purchasing foreign goods. Corruption in the customs service is rife, and most foreign companies work very closely with local partners to achieve success.

Foreign companies find it almost impossible to control prices, which are generally volatile. Some products are priced out of the market by arbitrary taxes.

Hungary

Hungary has only 10 million inhabitants, but it is rapidly becoming a base for the regional headquarters of multinationals (for instance General Motors, Compaq, and PepsiCo).

Distribution channels tend to be flat, with an importer/wholesaler directly supplying retail outlets. Budapest is dominated by large stores, but elsewhere small family-run shops are the norm. European chains have a strong presence, including Marks & Spencer, IKEA, and Metro. Checks are rarely used, but the country has a good ATM network.

As in other troubled economies, local firms lack capital and favor foreign suppliers that will offer good credit terms. European firms are typically offering 60 days' credit. Hungarian intermediaries tend to be small and often seek to act as agents, avoiding the need to finance stock purchases.

Trade shows, fairs, and seminars in association with local universities are effective promotional methods. Television and print advertising are considered to be very important.

Italy

Italy is a large and sophisticated market, moving from a highly fragmented distribution system serving small family-run stores and street vendors towards large supermarket chains. Sunday trading has been liberalized. High-volume/low-profit goods are often sold directly to large stores and chains by the manufacturer.

Restrictions on part-time employment make it difficult to operate a countrywide sales force. Mail order and catalogue sales are effective, but a poor postal service causes delays. This is likely to be improved by the advent of private delivery services.

Telephone direct marketing is effective for business-to-business sales, while consumers are responsive to the ubiquitous teleshopping TV channels.

After a slow start, Internet usage in Italy has experienced explosive growth since 1999. The number of business and home Internet users is booming: Internet users were estimated at over 12 million at the end of 2000, projected to reach 29 million by 2003. E-commerce is booming. Worth over $4bn in 2000, business-to-business e-commerce is well-established. Domestic PC penetration is low, with only around a third of Italian households having computer access, but e-sales of music, travel, and computer hardware and software are growing fast.

Japan

Japan's distribution system is fundamentally different from those in the industrialized West and is widely seen as a powerful unofficial trade barrier. Manufacturers control the channels through a large number of small intermediaries serving small retail outlets. Consumer goods commonly pass through four intermediaries to reach the customer. Middlemen are tied to the manufacturers by extended credit terms, generous rebates based on performance, an open returns policy, and intense promotional support.

KEY LEARNING POINTS

» Quality – let your customers tell you what they mean by "quality" and don't impose your own views. Low price and low maintenance are key factors in poorer countries.
» Packaging and labeling – these will almost certainly have to be adapted for each foreign market.
» Feet or meters? – it is an irony that the most economically powerful country in the world (the US) is having trouble adapting to the metric system. It's always painful to adapt, but in the long term a single global system of measurements benefits everyone.
» The ISO system – carefully analyze whether the potential benefits of ISO justify the investment of time and money in getting certification. The decision will vary from firm to firm.
» Global demand – business-to-business demand is generally more volatile than in consumer markets. Be very cautious about optimistic long-term projections of demand, especially in new and promising industries.
» Distribution methods vary enormously – study the target market's system carefully before entering.

» Use local staff – many firms first enter foreign markets by simply selling to an importer. As the business grows, the firm may set up a local subsidiary to maximize returns. Whatever arrangements you make for selling to a foreign market, the evidence shows overwhelmingly that it is essential to work closely with local people, both as employees of your own firm and as colleagues in other businesses.

NOTES

1 National Law Center for Inter-American Free Trade (1997) "Understanding Nom-050: a guide to Mexican consumer product labeling requirements." *Latin American Legal Developments Bulletin*, 5:3.
2 Zuckerman, A. (1994) "ISO 9000 skepticism." *Industry Week*, July 4.
3 David, L. (2000) "First Iridium satellite to tumble out of the sky," November 28. Available online at www.space.com

The State of the Art

» Cross-cultural communication.
» Update those phrase books!
» Defining the differences.
» Cross-cultural business-to-business negotiations.
» Bargaining tactics and behavior.
» Adapting the product.
» Corruption.
» Fraud.

"Behind every great fortune lies a crime."
Honoré de Balzac, Le Père Goriot, *1834*

CROSS-CULTURAL COMMUNICATION

We tend to have a much more sophisticated understanding of countries that have had a long and close association with our own – for example, the British are still the most common foreign travelers in India, the French are often highly knowledgeable about much of Africa, and many Americans have a good understanding of Latin America. It often comes as a surprise to Westerners to discover that people in other regions are far better informed about us than we are about them; it's a function of the West's success in dominating world business until very recently.

This kind of sophistication is not new – nineteenth-century European travelers to remote parts of Africa and Asia were often astonished to find that apparently isolated people were aware of political and business events in Western countries. Nor is it confined to developing countries; for example, a 1999 study found evidence that Japanese managers in international businesses were better informed about Australian national cultural values than their Australian counterparts were about Japan's.[1]

UPDATE THOSE PHRASE BOOKS!

It is important to appreciate that what once might have been a relatively accurate generalization may have now become a misleading stereotype. For example, US business textbooks and trade magazines still emphasize the differences between American and British use of language as if it is a serious barrier; warnings are issued that the British will misunderstand the meanings of words such as "stud," "billion," and "closet," and carefully explain that they are likely to talk to American colleagues about wearing "bathing dresses" and "keeping one's pecker up." The reality is that most British people know that one meaning of "stud" is a sexually vigorous male, call a thousand million a "billion" (formerly a billion was a million million), and know that "closet" means a cupboard or wardrobe – Americans who take the advice of one writer who states that "closet" usually refers to the WC will be met with blank looks in Britain. Expressions such as "bathing dresses" and "keeping one's pecker up" are anachronisms in the UK. Many language differences do still exist between the two nations, but there are also wide variations domestically. American accents and usage reach Britain through the media, as they do in most of the rest of the world. There's no doubt that this is a major change; the advent of talking pictures in 1929, still within living memory, astonished many Britons at the time, who had no idea of how Americans talked.

The point here is that the non-English speaking world has become remarkably familiar with Anglo-American style and culture over the last half century and is likely to make allowances for cultural gaffes – especially ones that commonly occur.

DEFINING THE DIFFERENCES

Anyone dealing with people from other countries tends to develop ideas about the differences in values and behaviors, but is doing this a form of prejudice? It's common, for instance, to hear talk of the "national character" of a certain group, and some feel that this may lead to useless or pejorative stereotyping.

Researchers Sudhir Kale and John Barnes argue that the idea of "national character" is a useful one, because "this construct incorporates both economic and cultural aspects and, as such, it is ideally suited to studying marketing exchanges."[2] Various scholarly attempts have been made to identify components of "national character" that can be measured objectively. Geert Hofstede proposes four dimensions.

1 **Uncertainty avoidance (UAI)** – how people in a particular society respond to uncertainty. High-UAI societies feel threatened by uncertainty, while low-UAI societies are accepting of it. Hofstede found that Japan, Belgium, and France were high-UAI societies, while Denmark, Sweden, and Hong Kong were low in UAI. The US was in the median range.
2 **Individualism (IDV)** – this is a measure of how much individual freedom prevails in a society. Some are "collectivist," expecting people to help one another, be strongly loyal to the group, and only hold beliefs and opinions that are acceptable to the group. At the other extreme, highly individualistic societies have nuclear families, expect people to take care of themselves, and value freedom in behavior as well as thought. Hofstede found that the UK, the US,

and Holland were high in IDV, while Pakistan, Taiwan, and Ecuador were low.

3 **Power distance (PDI)** – some countries allow differences in ability and opportunity to result in huge extremes in wealth and power, while others try to minimize it and strive for relative equality. Once again, the US fell between the two extremes, while France, India, and the Philippines had high PDI scores and Austria, Israel, and Denmark had low PDIs.

4 **Masculinity (MAS)** – MAS attempted to measure how far a society's behavior could be characterized as "masculine" (aggressive, assertive, money-chasing) or "feminine" (nurturing, caring, protecting). Japan, Italy, and Austria had high MAS, while Holland and the Scandinavian countries had low MAS.[3]

Clearly, if these findings hold true, they are important both to the introduction and promotion of products and to personal selling styles in different countries. An environmentally-friendly product, for instance, might have a higher chance of acceptance in a low-MAS country than in a high one, while Hofstede believes that hard-selling is ineffective in low-UAI cultures but may be acceptable in ones with high UAI. High-PDI countries such as Japan tend to regard salespeople as "little more than a beggar" and are mistrustful of strangers, so a humble relationship-building approach is appropriate.

CROSS-CULTURAL BUSINESS-TO-BUSINESS NEGOTIATIONS

Specialized cosmopolitan salespeople and deal-makers often say that they have to adapt their approaches radically when in different countries. Technology venture capitalist Fred Wilson of Flatiron Partners in New York says:

> "The one thing that is nice about Latin America is that it's really much simpler for us to do business there because there's no time difference. You can take an overnight flight and be in Buenos Aires in the morning – you are in the same time zone and culturally they're very similar, they're capitalists at heart, they've a very

similar value system and they're very interested in anything that's American.

"... the cultural gaps between the US and Asia are huge. Certain things, such as the act of managing an investment, are problematic. They're very concerned about the need to be respected and so you can't say to somebody, 'You're pissing me off!' Why can't I say that, if that's what I'm feeling? But no, you can't say that. How are we ever going to communicate? How can I tell them that I'm pissed off at them, that I feel I'm being screwed?

"In Latin America it's not like that, they're a little bit different but they are not as different. You can say, 'Look, I'm pissed off at you.' And they say, 'OK, so you're pissed off at me, I'm pissed off at you.'

"In Europe I think you can actually get away with the US style. If I go to the UK or France or Germany, they'll say, 'Oh, he's such an American,' but at least they can understand it. I guess there's been so much trade and business activity that they are used to us. You try to be on your best behavior, though."[4]

BARGAINING TACTICS AND BEHAVIOR

Writing in the *Journal of Marketing*, researcher Subhash Jain argues that marketing is the field where cross-cultural misunderstandings are most likely to occur,[5] a view supported by many other students of the subject. During the 1980s and 1990s, the problem received a great deal of academic attention, the purpose being to establish scientifically useful definitions of such notions as "national character," and to develop a clear understanding of how variations in corporate culture and individual behavior across the world affected business deals. Attention was paid to non-verbal behavior in meetings, which transmits much information below the level of awareness. A systematic study of business negotiations with participants from 15 different countries analyzed verbal and non-verbal communication by examining hours of videotape of simulated negotiations. Bargaining tactics and behavior were classified into a number of categories, such as how many times people said "No;" the number and length of silences; and the use of threats, interruption, warnings, questions, touching, promises, and so on. These categories were then used as scales against which the results from each group could be measured – for example, how often did Americans say "No" compared with the Japanese?

Though not conclusive, the following differences in the negotiating styles of various nationalities emerged.

Russia

Russians behaved distinctly differently from other Europeans, but had some remarkable similarities to the Japanese style, such as a reluctance to say "No" and "You." They used silence more than any other group, avoided "facial gazing," and asked a lot of questions.

Japan

The Japanese style was found to be "low on aggression," meaning that there was little use of threats, warnings, and commands, but many promises, commitments, and recommendations. Like the Russians, they were frequently silent, and avoided "facial gazing" and saying "No" and "You."

China

Regional differences in behavior within China are thought to be large. The study looked at negotiators from northern China and found that they had a similar style to the Japanese, except for asking many more questions.

South Korea

South Koreans were found to be more "aggressive" than the Japanese. They said "No" frequently, avoided silence, and were not afraid of interrupting.

Taiwan

The researchers concluded that the Taiwanese style was radically different from that of China and Japan, but had resemblances to the South Korean style. They used "facial gazing" more than any other group, volunteered more information than other Asians, and did not ask many questions.

Germany

Germans fell near the center of most of the scales, but were unusually high at self-disclosure (revealing information about themselves to their opposing negotiators). Also, they asked relatively few questions.

France

French negotiators were seen as the most "aggressive" of all, with frequent interruptions and use of "No" and "You."

Spain

The Spanish were the most frequent interrupters, and used many "commands" (defined as statements "in which the source suggests that the target perform a certain behavior").

UK

The study found that, on most scales, the score of British negotiators was very similar to that of the US negotiators.

Brazil

Brazilians were "aggressive," used many commands, said "No" and "You" frequently, and touched others several times.

Mexico

Mexicans behaved very differently from other Latin Americans, and were more like negotiators from the US.

Canada

English-speaking Canadians were the least aggressive of all the groups, while their French-speaking compatriots were highly aggressive and behaved in a similar way to the group from France.

US

US negotiators fell in the center of most scales, but interrupted the least of all.[6]

EXPLOITING CONCEPTS OF TIME – SOLAR TURBINES

The US firm Solar Turbines was negotiating with a Russian group over the sales of gas turbines and compressors to be used in a Russian pipeline. The concluding negotiations were held in the south of France, and Solar executives were astonished to find that the Russians seemed entirely unwilling to talk business. After a few days, they guessed what was happening – the Russian group wanted to enjoy their time in France and didn't want to cut their trip short. Persuading Solar's head office to give them time, the Americans sat back and waited, limiting business to short morning meetings that left the rest of the day free for the Russians to play golf, shop, and lie on the beach. Three weeks passed pleasantly and, in the fourth, the Russians suddenly became eager to do business. The reason? They could not return to Moscow without a deal, having spent a month on the Côte d'Azur!

ADAPTING THE PRODUCT

Here's a brief look at some of the main factors that create the need to adapt products for specific markets.

Packaging and labeling

» Packaging often has to be changed to conform to a country's regulations, but cultural factors have to be considered too. In countries with low levels of literacy, pictures and symbols on packets are often instructions for use, and an overly decorated package may be ignored because consumers do not know what is inside.

» The size of the package is also a key factor in low-income mass markets where people can only afford to buy small quantities of a product: Wrigley's sells single sticks of chewing gum in China, for example, while Sunsilk shampoo is sold in individual sachets in India.

» As in the West, the color pink is associated with girls in China. A case of easy cultural translation, then? Not so – Procter & Gamble's pink packages of diapers failed in China because people prefer to have boys, not girls, and do not want to lose face by others seeing the package and assuming that they have a girl child.

PRODUCTS CAN BE UPWARDLY OR DOWNWARDLY MOBILE AROUND THE WORLD.

Thunderbird, an American fortified apple wine often associated with skid row in the US, sells as a popular middle-class drink in Malaysia. Malaysia taxes alcohol made from grapes at a much higher rate than if it is made from other fruit, so Thunderbird is cheaper in Malaysia than the cheapest of wines, while its sweet taste appeals to local palates. In Islamic tradition, drinking grape wine is often seen as more of a transgression than other forms of alcohol, which contributes to Thunderbird's success among liberal Malays.

Instructions

We've all struggled with incomprehensible instruction leaflets that come with electrical goods from the Far East, so it should not be surprising that many non-English speakers have difficulty in understanding the instructions on many British and American products. Apparently simple directions such as "danger" or "use no oil" will not be understood by non-English speakers.

Stereotypes, ethnocentrism, and national pride

We might like to believe that simple-minded prejudices are rapidly becoming a thing of the past, but international selling must respond to local realities if it is to succeed. In many countries, specific types of products are associated with particular countries that are thought to produce the best quality – for example English tea, French scent, Italian leather, and so on are widely regarded as the best. The most industrialized nations tend to have a competitive advantage over others in many third-world countries because their products are perceived as having high quality simply because of their origin. In Russia, people prefer locally produced food but want imported clothes and consumer durables. Brands are less important than the country of origin, and locally made Polaroid cameras and Philips irons have not been successful.

National brands

Unilever has a strategy of mixing global and national brands. In Poland, for example, it introduced Omo washing powder, but also purchased the local product Pollena 2000. Polish consumers showed a preference for the local brand which soon won the lion's share of the market, defeating Omo and its foreign rival Ariel (owned by Procter & Gamble).

Private brands

Global manufacturers' brands have been losing ground in recent years to "private" brands owned by local retailers, particularly in Europe. National food retailers wield a lot of power in their territories, and are able to control shelf display and prices to favor their own brands. In the UK, the Sainsbury food chain's own brands typically make up around half of the total product range in its stores and account for two-thirds of its sales. Private food brands have 30% of the UK and Swiss markets, and 20% in France and Germany. Price is a factor – global manufacturers' brands tend to have a premium price, and national chains are able to offer own-brand products of equivalent quality more cheaply.

GOING INTERNATIONAL? – MAYBE IT'S TIME TO CHANGE THE BRAND NAME

We've all heard amusing stories of blunders made by multinationals when introducing products to foreign markets, such as the launch of the Ford Pinto in Brazil, where *pinto* can mean a small penis, but it is remarkable how many national product names have inappropriate meanings in other languages. Here are a few from around the world that would be greeted with hilarity by English-speaking consumers:

» Poo – curry powder, Argentina;
» Mukk – yogurt, Italy;
» Fart – household cleanser, Poland;
» Crapsy Fruit – cereal, France;
» Bimbo – bread, Spain and Mexico;
» Kack – confectionery, Denmark; and
» Pocari Sweat – chocolate, Japan.

A toothpaste that used to be sold widely in South Asia under the brand name "Darkie" featured the picture of a man of African origin with shiny white teeth. In the 1980s, in response to concerns that this was offensive, the brand name was changed to "Darlie."

Climate and topography

Variations in climate around the world have both obvious and subtle effects on selling in different countries. Many products have to be adapted for different climates, even within a single national market. For example, washing machine manufacturers give their products a spin cycle that is up to three times faster in northern Europe than in Mediterranean countries, because clothes are less frequently hung outside to dry in the north and therefore need to come out drier from the washing machine. Most heavy machinery is originally constructed to function well in temperate climates, and must be modified to cope with the extremes of heat and dust to be found in countries such as Saudi Arabia. In Singapore, the country with the most lightning in the world, computer users install circuit-breakers as standard equipment to prevent data loss and other damage when lightning strikes nearby.

In South America, most of the population is concentrated in cities, widely dispersed, and separated by awesome natural barriers. In Colombia, the trip from Bogotá to Medellín takes half an hour by air, but up to 12 hours by road across a high mountain range. Marketers generally divide the country into four territories, reflecting their very different climates and lifestyles.

CORRUPTION

It's embarrassing, unpleasant, and nobody wants to talk about it, but if you are involved in international sales, you will almost certainly encounter it. Making payments to government officials and corporate employees is a simple fact of life in many countries. You may think that the superiority of your product and your skillful closing techniques will make the sale – but perhaps your competitors know better.

What's more, firms from the most developed countries seem to be perfectly willing to pay bribes, despite having laws against doing so in their home countries. According to Peter Eigen, Chairman of Transparency International, a global anti-corruption non-governmental organization, there can be "no doubt that large numbers of multinational corporations from the richest nations are pursuing a criminal course to win contracts in the leading emerging market economies of the world . . . The governments of the richest nations continue to fail to recognize the rampant undermining of fair global trade by bribe-paying multinational enterprises."[7]

Until recently, it was virtually taboo to discuss corruption in business or official circles. In the early 1990s, however, the Organization for Economic Cooperation and Development (OECD) began to campaign against corruption, and by 1997 most Western countries had agreed to an OECD Convention on Combating Bribery of Foreign Public Officials in International Business Transactions.[8]

EU law

Most European countries have laws against corruption, both at home and abroad, but there are loopholes – for instance, bribes to foreigners are still generally tax-deductible and can be included in export credit insurance. There are now a number of initiatives within the EU to stamp out bribes to foreigners as part of a wider drive to increase transparency in overseas aid and trade.

The scale of the problem can be appreciated from the recent revelations about Elf, formerly a state-owned oil company in France that is now privatized.

ELF

Elf, the French oil company, is the subject of a long-running series of scandals relating to bribes paid to French and German politicians as well as to officials in poorer countries. The "affaire Dumas" came to light when it was found that a senior employee of Elf, Christine Deviers-Joncour, paid her lover, French Foreign Office Minister Roland Dumas, some £6.5mn to approve the 1991 sale of six frigates to Taiwan in which Elf had a financial interest. Dumas was jailed for six months and fined 1 million francs (approximately £100,000).

It then transpired that Elf's number two, Alfred Sirven, had been in charge of the systematic bribery (estimated at £300mn) to European and African officials – other senior French politicians, such as Edith Cresson, who is alleged to have received £60,000 for "advice," were implicated. In 2000, Elf was found by a Swiss magistrate to have paid bribes to German officials and political parties to obtain German government subsidies for the purchase of Leuna, an East German oil refiner.

The US

During the 1970s, the US stock market regulator, the Securities and Exchange Commission, found that more than 400 major firms admitted making payments to officials, politicians, and political parties in foreign countries. The total amount of bribes was estimated to be more than $300mn.

As a response to these revelations, and as part of the general drive for reform following the Watergate scandal, the US Foreign Corrupt Practices Act (FCPA) became law in 1977. The FCPA banned firms that issue shares on US stock markets from bribing foreign officials, and tightened up accounting rules so as to make bribe payments more difficult to disguise.

There is one major exception, however. "Facilitating payments" for "routine governmental action" are explicitly allowed. For example, it is legal to pay bribes to foreign officials for permits and licenses; processing governmental papers; providing police protection; postal, telephone, electricity, and water services; and loading and unloading cargo. But, bribing an official to obtain new business or continue business is specifically excluded from the "facilitating payment" definition.

The FCPA also provides for an "affirmative defense" that a bribe was permitted by the foreign country's laws, or that the money was spent as part of demonstrating a product or performing a contractual obligation, but the onus is on the defendant to prove that this was the case.[9]

The law affects the many foreign companies that issue securities in the US – most major UK firms, for example, do this in addition to their listing on the London stock market. Since 1998, the FCPA also applies to foreign firms and nationals who pay bribes in US territory.

In addition, the act covers joint ventures and subsidiaries in foreign countries.

Less than 50 prosecutions have been made under the FCPA, but a few convictions have been obtained and a handful of company employees have been jailed.

Who pays bribes?

According to surveys, many large firms do. One such survey was conducted by Gallup on behalf of Transparency International, and culminated in the release of the Bribe Payers Index 2002[10] (Table 6.1).

Table 6.1 Bribe Payers Index 2002.

Rank	Country	Score
1	Australia	8.5
2	Sweden	8.4
3	Switzerland	8.4
4	Austria	8.2
5	Canada	8.1
6	Netherlands	7.8
7	Belgium	7.8
8	UK	6.9
9	Singapore	6.3
10	Germany	6.3
11	Spain	5.8
12	France	5.5
13	US	5.3
14	Japan	5.3
15	Malaysia	4.3
16	Hong Kong	4.3
17	Italy	4.1
18	South Korea	3.9
19	Taiwan	3.8
20	China	3.5
21	Russia	3.2
	Domestic companies	1.9

Source: Transparency International, survey by Gallup.

The survey was given to senior executives of domestic and foreign companies, chartered accountants, bankers, commercial lawyers, and other business leaders in the following 15 emerging market nations: Argentina, Brazil, Colombia, Hungary, India, Indonesia, Mexico, Morocco, Nigeria, the Philippines, Poland, Russia, South Africa, South Korea, and Thailand. These countries have very large trade and investment business with multinational firms. A total of 835 interviews were carried out between December 2001 and March 2002.

The questions in the survey were concerned with how respondents perceived the activities of multinational firms from 21 countries. The ranking of multinationals by country emerged from answers to the question, "In the business sectors with which you are most familiar, please indicate how likely companies from the following countries are to pay or offer bribes to win or retain business in this country?" Ranks are based on scores of 0 to 10 (where 0 = a very high perceived willingness to pay bribes and 10 = no perceived willingness to pay bribes).

Since the sample is relatively small and the survey relates to perceptions, the exact score is probably less important that the order of ranking; for example, it is meaningless to say that Spain's score of 5.8 shows that its multinationals are 0.5 more corrupt than Germany's (which scored 6.3), but it is meaningful to say that multinationals from, say, Russia, China, and Taiwan were perceived as being considerably more willing to pay bribes than multinationals from Australia, Sweden, and Switzerland.

To the uninitiated, most shocking of all is the fact that multinationals from the major Western nations were all regarded as willing to pay bribes to some degree.

FRAUD

Companies are generally alert to fraud, especially when dealing with new overseas customers, but international business naturally increases the risks. Here's one disturbing phenomenon that affects smaller firms.

Nigerian advance-fee fraud

From Massachusetts to Malaysia, business people and professionals of many nationalities have suffered serious losses and even death at the hands of a remarkable web of fraudsters originating from Nigeria. Difficult to catch because of their loose, non-hierarchical organization – typically any individual can be the boss of a scam that he or she originates – these sophisticated fraudsters operate all around the world, preying on people's eagerness for "windfall" profits.

Although the variations of the scam are endless and are becoming ever-more creative, the basic proposition is as follows. You are contacted by letter, fax, or email from an individual claiming to be an employee of the Nigerian government, a Nigerian bank, an associate of some powerful African political figure, or an established African firm. The bait is money – often a huge sales contract or a hefty commission for assistance in releasing blocked funds. Other deals include:

» help in transferring funds from "over-invoiced" or "over-estimated" contracts;
» offering crude oil at low prices; and
» help in transferring the assets of deposed leaders abroad.

Often the letters contain crude spelling mistakes and other errors designed to make the recipient feel a sense of superiority. Although the proposition is often obviously illegal, there are also versions that appear above board, such as a sales contract, a bequest to a charity, or a scholarship.

What happens next depends upon your response. The fraudster needs to know your preferences and how much cash you have access to. While low-level fraudsters will be satisfied with taking a relatively small amount of money (for example, by asking for a $1000 "advance fee" to help move the process along), master fraudsters will go to extraordinary lengths to convince you that the deal is genuine. With trade deals, there have been many cases where there have been a series of transactions increasing in value – the foreign supplier is paid on time until the last, big deal when no payment is forthcoming. According to the US Embassy in Lagos, 50% of all Federal Express, UPS, and DHL shipments to Nigeria are returned because of fraud and theft.

In other cases foreigners have been brought to Nigeria, all expenses paid, to have meetings with genuine Nigerian government officials in government offices during office hours. Genuine-looking documents are invariably forthcoming.

With the increasing publicity about these scams, more and more fraudsters are basing their deal in neighbouring countries such as Benin and Ghana, and often claim not to be Nigerian.

KEY LEARNING POINTS

» Cultural differences manifest themselves in dissimilar ways in business and consumer markets. While business customers may be better informed and more sophisticated about your own culture, their own organizational culture may force them to behave in unexpected ways. Hofstede's PDI scale, for example, reminds us that there are many countries that have very "undemocratic" ideas about social status. Ignoring such factors could prove disastrous.

» Local brands may be preferred over international ones in some countries; multinationals are responding to this by purchasing local brands and marketing them alongside their own global products. Powerful retailers in Europe are experiencing success in marketing own-brand products of a similar quality to competing global brands, but at a lower price.

» What is seen as corruption in one country may be everyday practice in another. Currently there is an international drive to reduce corruption in business, but it is generally recognized that there is an ethical difference between "facilitating payments," amounting to "tips," and true bribery, which is thought to be damaging to all firms in the long run.

» High-level corruption occurs in all countries, not just in the developing world. Owing to national security issues, the arms trade is particularly susceptible to corrupt practices.

NOTES

1 Soutar, G.N., Grainger, R., & Hedges, P. (1999) "Australian and Japanese value stereotypes: a two-country study." *Journal of International Business Studies*, first quarter, pp. 203–16.

2 Kale, S.H. & Barnes, J.W. (1992) "Understanding the domain of cross-national buyer–seller interactions." *Journal of International Business Studies*, first quarter, pp. 101–32.

3 Hofstede, G. (1980) *Culture's Consequences: International differences in work-related values*. Sage Publications, Beverly Hills, CA.

4 Gough, L. (2000) *Investing in Internet Stocks*. John Wiley & Sons, Chichester.

5 Jain, S.C. (1989) "Standardization of international marketing strategy: some research hypotheses." *Journal of Marketing*, **53**:1, pp. 70-9.

6 Caterora, P.R. & Graham, J.L. (2002) *International Marketing* (11th edn), Chapter 19. McGraw-Hill, Boston.

7 Statement by Peter Eigen on the launch of the Bribe Payers Index 2002. Reported online at www.transparency.org

8 The OECD Convention on Combating Bribery of Foreign Public Officials in International Business Transactions came into force in February 1999. Further details may be found at www1.oecd.org/daf/nocorruption/ref.htm

9 Available online at www.usdoj.gov/criminal/fraud/fcpa/

10 Available online at www.transparency.org

In Practice – Global Sales Success Stories

» McDonald's – the mixed blessing of success.
» Check Point – mastering indirect sales.
» Samsung – bringing it all together.

"It is not in my view defamatory to say that the Plaintiffs use gimmicks. Many marketing companies do so, and I do not believe that this on its own would lower either Plaintiff in the estimation of reasonable people."

Mr Justice Bell, summarizing his verdict on June 19, 1997, in a
libel case between McDonald's and activists Helen Steel and
David Morris

MCDONALD'S – THE MIXED BLESSING OF SUCCESS

What do you do to boost sales for a brand that becomes too successful? Somehow, during the late 1990s, McDonald's became a brand even more identified with American-style capitalism than the previous standard-bearer, Coca-Cola. This identification turned out to be a mixed blessing after McDonald's restaurants were trashed in Paris or vilified by demonstrators against globalization in the streets of Seattle. The chain suffered six consecutive quarterly declines in earnings to mid-2002, and was reeling from accusation after accusation in a chain of bad publicity that started with something it was not at all responsible for: BSE, or "mad cow disease."

It did not seem that way in the late 1990s, when the opening of another branch in Belarus could be the cause of enthusiastic riots. Or when 30,000 people stood in line to buy and eat food at the opening of the chain's new restaurant in Chengdu, China, in 1999. The sales strategy of a chain this size – in which over 70% of the business is managed by franchisees – is of necessity more of a marketing and brand management story. But the chain's meticulous attention to the detail of selling in every store, down to the level of how to display every poster, creates a continuum between marketing and sales that makes it interesting, both when it works and when it needs fixing.

The 1990s were the years of global expansion for the "Golden Arches" as franchises were opened in country after country in Eastern Europe, the Far East, and the Middle East, and with more countries in Latin America joining the McUniverse. The simple secret was that there was nothing more people in these new markets wanted than a good old American/global hamburger with standardized fries. When merchandized goods from Disney movies accompanied the fries, the recipe was perfect because it was new, clean, and, well, McDonald's.

In many of these new markets, nobody had ever thought of enticing families to eat at a restaurant by giving presents to the children. That's not the way things work in traditional societies, but the purveyors of global brands are very aware of the key secret that few traditional societies want to stay that way.

A key ingredient of the secret sauce of the 1990s was that the omnipresent global hamburger was always available, but the restaurants were less global than they seemed. In India, people who make and handle veggie burgers work in a different area and wear differently colored uniforms to assuage any concerns of the most rigorous vegetarian. In Egypt, the Big Mac can be accompanied by the Mu'allim or The Boss, a Mcdonaldized form of falafel (a chickpea rissole), while the burgers in Hong Kong are slathered in a black pepper sauce. Some products are launched locally for a potential world audience, while others are completely local. In South America, for example, items like the McNifica were developed in Argentina and then moved to other Latin American countries. The McRuis, a rye-based bun, on the other hand was developed in Finland with no plans to export it anywhere else.

Despite the ubiquitous colors and uniformity of McDonald's restaurants, the franchisees in various countries also had a lot to say for themselves, both in terms of business structure and brand identification. By and large, McDonald's traditional preference for individual franchisees – people as opposed to companies – has proved itself especially in new markets because of the individual responsibility and the sensibility to local concerns.

The new franchises were generally happy because the marketing support from McDonald's is both constant and dynamic, and is usually promoted in an annual sales cycle that used symbiotic but temporary co-branding with media products from Hollywood. McDonald's probably defined co-branding for all times in its relationship with Coca-Cola. But the support Coke and McDonald's extend to each other is static. A hot movie or television link is a dynamic sales strategy because it can and should ride every success story in the market.

Globally it makes sense because it allows the launch of global campaigns to encourage each market before and during the key summer season, working well with local franchisees' incentive schemes or lotteries. Children are on holiday in the summer, movies are made for children, and McDonald's meals are made for children clamoring for media products based on the movies. Media co-branding is also flexible – movies like *Mulan* were co-marketed globally, while franchisees could also make more local links like the Brazilian franchisees did with the Disney movie *Atlantis*.

The company's Serbian operation responded masterfully to the problems presented by NATO's bombing of Serbia in 1999. The Golden Arches trademark was topped with a traditional Serbian cap, a nationalist symbol, and anti-NATO demonstrators in Belgrade were given 3000 free burgers. Signs in the restaurants emphasized that they "shared in Serbian destiny" and reminded customers that their restaurants, too, could be bombed. A long-running program of sponsorship of schools and hospitals also helped to maintain a positive image.

Funnily enough, when the trend towards increased localization and co-branding was being polished to perfection, McDonald's started to hurt in the key markets where people bought hamburgers not because they were glamorous – like in the third world – but because they were a fact of life.

The first big blow was the BSE scandal in Europe. McDonald's could have dozens of vegetarian, chicken, or fish products, but beef was and is the heart of the business. BSE made customers feel that there was something wrong with the products McDonald's desperately needed to have perceived as good and wholesome.

If BSE was not enough, a slew of nasty publicity in Britain and other countries seriously tarnished the portrait of good corporate citizenship that the corporation and its franchises had worked so hard to create. Then there were allegations that McDonald's foods were not healthy for children. These were hard to counter because people tend not to believe corporate denials about food products. Some of the bad publicity was plain silly, like a claim that the tartan design the chain used for the uniforms of employees in British restaurants belonged to the Clan Lindsay, and not McDonald. Even this was hard to digest in a corporation that had fostered a diet of the blandest possible positive image.

It was a series of blows to a huge business, in which image was just as important as food. As of mid-2002, there were over 30,000 McDonald's restaurants in over 120 countries in the world. The worst damage in Europe had been stemmed, but the brand was still leaking energy in the Far East and not showing dynamic growth in any important market machine.

The ingredients of the new strategy are complex. Some are direct responses to criticism, like two separate decisions regarding the key children's market. In terms of product the chain introduced larger meals for slightly older children. After a year, it addressed its perceptions of their parents' health concerns by introducing supposedly healthier yoghurt-based products as well. At the same time, the chain is continuing intensive localization with campaigns to introduce Indian-flavored food into British restaurants, for example.

The real challenge, however, is in the competition. Competitors like Burger King and Kentucky Fried Chicken use all the sales and marketing tricks that made the McDonald's concept so ubiquitous. Something new was needed to head them off. The company was looking for ways to adapt and change the winning formula of a self-service store with a lot of plastic and bright colors to a more adult concept that relied less on the fickle tastes of children. The first of these was the diner-inside concept – a full-service diner modeled on the American model of the 1950s. The second is the McCafé, which has been around under several names for the past decade or so but was not promoted on a global basis.

Somehow, something seemed to be working. By mid-2002 its sales figures had shown a slight improvement in the key American and European markets, while Asia was still in trouble. The challenge then was to find a global answer to reduce exposure to bad publicity while getting back on the path to sales growth. But that would only happen when the world economy got back on its feet.

KEY INSIGHTS

» For a global, highly standardized brand, McDonald's is a champion at changing menus and marketing concepts to suit local tastes.

» Global growth was relatively easy during the 1990s because people all over the less developed parts of the world welcomed McDonald's entrance to the market as a sign of progress.

> » Co-branding and merchandizing with media products give a crucial annual boost to sales as well as reinforcing the tie with the essential children's market. Developing menus that the children like and the parents approve of will be a key element in the chain's success.
> » McDonald's has had trouble defending itself because its image is so bland that it cannot react sharply to criticism.
> » The company's exposure to bad publicity is a real liability, which it needs to resolve. Its experience in Serbia, however, shows that it is capable of responding skillfully to potentially very serious problems.

CHECK POINT – MASTERING INDIRECT SALES

How do you maintain some of the best margins in the software business with a 100% indirect sales model? That question is the lifeblood of Check Point Software Technologies (NASDAQ: CHKP), the company that invented the firewall and dominates the world market for enterprise firewall software and virtual private networks (VPNs).

The sales model chosen by Check Point, a company based in Ramat Gan, Israel, is a classic example of making the very best of your disadvantages. Its current CEO, Gil Shwed, and two other partners founded the company in 1993. To reach the market, they raised a paltry $400,000 in venture finance, finished developing their very first product, and got on a plane to show it off in a trade show in the US, where they promptly won the best-of-the-show award.

The next breakthrough in 1994 was an agreement with Sun Microsystems to market Check Point's firewall, because no other company had an easily configurable way to protect corporate networks in these very early days of the commercial Internet. Exiting solutions were clunky and hard to install.

Even as some companies like Sun realized the need for the product, there is no way the tiny team in Israel could have created a sales and marketing presence in the US. At the beginning of its saga, the Check Point offices in the US were an empty office with an answering machine. As time went on and the company prospered, there were people in the US office – but not salespeople.

These modest beginnings led to a company that commanded net earnings of $322mn on sales of $528mn in fiscal 2001. A network of over 2500 integrators, distributors, and partners of various kinds made all these sales. In 2002, most estimates said that Check Point had reached a 60% market share of the enterprise firewall market and close to that share of the large corporate market for VPNs. VPNs are software programs that allow companies to create a secure channel of communications between corporate branches using the open (and insecure) Internet instead of expensive dedicated lines. VPNs are very likely to spell the end of dedicated lines for many companies, and thus affect the entire telecom market.

Four strategic factors were key elements of the environment in which Check Point developed its US sales strategy.

1 The company did not, and could not, have the resources to compete with its own sales staff in the crucial American market.
2 Computer security is a complicated business and, as such, creates ample room for value-added resellers (VARs) beside traditional distributors, solution providers, and all the other intermediaries in the business.
3 These intermediaries would only trust a vendor who devoted massive resources to R & D, because they need to know the next generation is always on its way.
4 The security business lives off paranoia and reputations – a company's name and image are of extreme importance because that is part of the assurance customers want and need.

The software business is a notoriously winner-takes-all market, with the market leader commanding margins two or three times better than their closest competitor. It is these margins that allow the market leader to invest more in R & D and brand-building, making the lead all the more impregnable.

To make the intermediaries' lives easier, Check Point devoted considerable resources to building its brand, through astute use of technological leadership and smart public relations. Check Point's name became associated with the best state-of-the-art defenses for corporate networks – a factor that became increasingly important over the years as executives began to feel the vulnerability that was, is, and always will be the price of better networks and more integrated global operations. Intermediaries knew that it was safe to recommend a Check Point firewall or VPN.

One of the most important solutions that Check Point gave these intermediaries and partners was a platform and standard for integrated Internet security. This standard is called OPSEC (Open Platform for Security), and is in effect a Check Point-dominated alliance of 300 vendors of security products that guarantee interoperability. This level of interoperability removed a lot of the guesswork for the VARs and other players in the field who were actually selling security products and systems. Naturally, they would prefer applications with tested and guaranteed interoperability, and just as naturally they would choose Check Point products for their customers.

OPSEC not only gave a level of comfort to Check Point's indirect salespeople – it solidified its lead in a market where technological leadership is taken seriously because of the always rising level of threat to corporate networks. OPSEC gives the actual sellers the knowledge and assurance that somebody out there is working not only on the individual product but also on integrating the entire package they are presenting to their customer. OPSEC is the bridgehead into new markets as well, with Check Point using it for the foray into mobile markets it started in 2002.

The issue of technological leadership is critical in this market. The cat-and-mouse game played between the hackers and companies that protect networks is a never-ending war in which both sides need new tools and methods all of the time. Companies need to be perceived as reliable technology leaders – the kind of image that both Check Point and Symantec – the world leaders in anti-virus software – cultivate so assiduously.

The high point of the year in terms of showing this leadership is the Check Point Experience, a developer, partner, and customer convention held in the US, Europe, and Asia. In 2002, these events were used to launch new products, including a series that requires constant updates like an anti-virus program – a move into the recurring-revenue business model of selling subscription services.

These events will become even more important as Check Point moves into its next markets. The total world market for security products and services in 2001 was estimated at $8bn, and nearly all analysts expect this figure to grow dramatically over the next few years. Much of this market is for services of the kind sold by the software intermediaries Check Point needs to sell its products. Check Point might be the major player in the market but there is still a lot of room for consolidation – as well as fending off the threat from the behemoth of the software and hardware business.

In software, Microsoft started to incorporate firewalls into its XP operating system and, even though this has not created an impact on sales in mid-2002, nobody can afford to take a threat from Microsoft lightly. In hardware, the threat comes from Cisco Corp., which sells firewall products embedded into its hardware. People like boxes – as distinct from Check Point's pure software protection. Check Point has faced and overcome this challenge from Cisco, but this is one of the reasons Check Point entered into partnership with Nokia to sell firewalls embedded into Nokia's Ipsilon boxes that act like very fast routers.

The partnership with Nokia answered Check Point's need to work with established sales channels, but it did not develop quickly enough. The distributors' VARs and other indirect salespeople were clamoring for a good product to compete in the lower end of the market. So Check Point started to roll out boxes developed by its SofaWare subsidiary as cheap protection for smaller businesses. These boxes cannot possibly command the same kind of margin as high-end products, but it's what the people in the field want so it's what they get.

The challenge Check Point faced in 2002 – a difficult year by all accounts – was to find ways to retain its high margins in a recessionary market while expanding its reach into the mobile and low-end markets. In addition, it had to defend its reputation as the vendor of top-of-the-line products while aggressively pushing a cheaper product line through its sales channels. The challenge – and opportunity – of the short-range Wi-Fi (wireless-fidelity) markets will be the company's next test. Fortunately, its incredible margins created cash flow reserves that could make this possible.

KEY INSIGHTS

» The indirect sales development strategy is the only possible route for a poorly funded company from a small country that wanted to dominate the US market in a specific sector.

» Indirect sales allow Check Point to concentrate on what it is best at - R & D and brand-building. But the margins and shareholder value created by this pattern are most viable only for a market leader. The cruel paradox is that you can stay there only if you got there in the first place.

» High-powered R & D is critical for Check Point's indirect sales model - not only as a means of maintaining technological leadership, but also to maintain the equally important impression of technological leadership.

» Standards, alliances, and partnerships like OPSEC work because they give both customers and integrators the assurance they can get end-to-end solutions.

» Check Point works for its indirect salespeople, not only by boosting the brand, but by creating a situation in which the indirect sellers stand to make a lot of money by selling Check Point products.

SAMSUNG – BRINGING IT ALL TOGETHER

First there was Motorola, a brand that drove sales and had a major part in starting the cellular revolution. Then there was Ericsson, Siemens, and a few other players till Nokia made it clear that it was here to rule the cellular world.

Then, as the markets started to crash and it was clear that growth numbers of the cellular bonanza were running out, Samsung suddenly started to look like the only company that could seriously challenge the Finnish master of the cellular handset world.

The story of the Korean conglomerate's sales success after the stock/tech bubble burst is a classic story of great management orchestrating the complex factors needed to assault and succeed in complex markets with new kinds of consumer electronics.

At least one of the factors that helped Samsung was negative – the Asian meltdown of 1997 created reasons for radical change while US and European companies were settling into the ramp-up of the bubble. Others were governmental – the Korean government's decision to invest heavily in broadband and mobile technology created the world's most vibrant lab for communications technologies and markets. Other reasons were corporate – Samsung seems to be one of these companies where the word synergy is not a tired cliché, as various divisions across Samsung Electronics really do cooperate in creating the best cutting-edge computing communications and entertainment gizmos. Then there is there is the issue of global roll-out on five continents, three cellular technologies, and broadband standards leaving enough room for localization. Integrate that with timely help in content development for cellular providers, and finally add heavy and highly successful investments in branding. It all adds up – doesn't it?

The checklist starts with a company that did not look so stellar in the dark days of 1997 when the Korean system of *chaebol* with intertwined companies and spiraling liabilities looked like it was going to bring down one of the great east Asian success stories. It didn't because the government was smart, the people hard-working, and mainly because companies like Samsung realized they had to reinvent themselves at once.

At the time, few people had heard of Samsung mobile phones outside of Korea, and Nokia was the company to notice as it started to reap the results of massive penetration of mobile phones in Europe and the US. The immediate priority in 1997 was to cut costs and increase sales. But Samsung Electronics CEO Yun Jong Yong had a tremendous advantage. While he was creating the fiscal discipline that saved the company, he had a wonderful tech-crazy home market. Market research suggests that an incredible 56% of all Koreans have cellphones. They also upgrade to a new model after nine months or so and are willing to try out innovative content in a way that only the Japanese can hope to match.

This home market creates a massive sales advantage for a cellular phone manufacturer. Relatively few cellular phones are sold directly to consumers. Most are distributed by cellular network operators or third-party chains. Perceptions of what the customer wants are critical, and Korean companies like Samsung have a major advantage in that they can bring out tested products that work well with the cellular providers' main concern, which is to enable features attractive enough for them to sell more airtime.

From the first minutes one held a Palm Pilot, it was clear that it should be a phone too. Samsung was one of the first actually to manufacture large amounts of personal digital assistant (PDA) phones, because it had the resources to combine the screen and phone technology in a design the customers liked. The ability to integrate semiconductor, communication, and screen technologies was and will be a critical element in the coming cellular battles after the year 2002, when screens go colored and broadband leaks into the mass market beyond the Far East. This depth of technology is a critical element in selling mobile phones, because companies who seek world leadership have to present different systems in regional markets in both the various versions of code-division multiple access (CDMA) and the successors to the global system for mobile communications (GSM).

Typically, in countries like Spain, localization is based on the assumption that people really do behave differently with their phones in different markets. GSM phones for the European and Mediterranean markets are manufactured in Spain close to the market where understanding of the model strategy is clear to everybody throughout the organization. The results are clear – being close to the market brought Samsung both brand recognition and sales first in Spain and then in other nearby markets.

In another Mediterranean market, Israel, Samsung faced the ultimate challenge of three separate networks working with three different technologies – GSM, CDMA and TDMA (time-division multiple access). The strategy used in this case was simple and effective. A large number of models was first introduced into the relatively small CDMA network (of the kind Samsung has in its home market) where they won recognition for their small size and superior characteristics. This set the stage for introducing models into the GSM market, and finally moving in with a limited number of models into the largest network that uses the relatively rare TDMA technology. No other country has the same set-up, and the sales strategy was intensely localized, with marketing and advertising kicking in as the sales expanded into larger networks.

More significantly, executives in cellular companies in Europe and the Mediterranean realized they could count on Samsung as they navigated the next stages in developing their markets. In mid-2002, it was clear that there were three separate and yet intertwined elements that could make for the next leap ahead in cellular sales in those markets that were already saturated. These three elements are colored screens; broadband or semi-broadband enabled content; or phone features like PDAs, music, or cameras embedded in the cellphone.

These factors are of critical importance to Samsung, which by the year 2001 had significantly eclipsed Nokia in the dollar value of handhelds it sold in the US market (though not in the number of units). Samsung wants to retain its high cost per set, and the cellular providers need to sell more airtime. The amount of help cellular providers get in setting up content management systems has become one part of the package that helps Samsung persuade the provider to push its sets.

By early 2002, Samsung was ready with a dazzling number of sets with all the advanced features that could meet each of these future growth opportunities. This capacity is of critical importance to cellular providers – most of whom have the heavy debt loads typical of the telecom market and the concomitant need to expand revenues with new services that can be rolled out easily. A phone executive is always most comfortable if their network is connected to a manufacturer that can rapidly supply the latest fad.

The last and possibly one of the most important elements is branding. Korean companies got the reputation for selling cheap me-too products in the 1980s – especially as they typically invested so heavily as to create overcapacity and subsequent sales at low, barely profitable prices. By the mid-1990s, Korea's heavy investment in plant and in education started to bear fruit, and companies like Samsung started to lead in innovation both in products and in patents. What was missing was the intangible element that allows companies with good innovative products to command higher returns on their investment. Or, put in blunt terms, Samsung had to learn how to be Sony, and get that automatic X percent premium on the sticker.

There are two parts of this strategy. The first is the product level, with heavy investments in design. The teenager gamer and harried executive both buy design, consciously and avidly. The second element is brand awareness, which took central place in the company's $900mn marketing budget for the year 2002. The investment in brand is crucial as the market faces the upgrade decisions of each individual consumer and entire networks. In this sense Samsung was just taking a page out of Nokia's book, but since it really had much more to offer than Nokia from the best flat-screens to mobile phones, the job of market leadership branding could be as effective as it is for Sony, a company that leads so many products under a strong brand. Samsung has made it clear that it wants to beat Sony not only on product, but also on brand. That's Korean ambition.

KEY INSIGHTS

» Managing sales growth in a global market for technology-intensive goods is a highly complex process that stretches over several years of constant preparation and execution.

» The existence of the vibrant, technologically sophisticated home market was a critical element of Samsung's success. The competition with other Korean companies and the willingness of Korean consumers frequently to upgrade mobile phones were critically important for the company. The most demanding tests were at home.

» The degree of localization was critically important – even in technology-intensive markets.

» Investments in branding can be even more helpful to companies with a broad product range. In simple terms, Nokia's branding simply helps it sell more telephones. Samsung's branding help's hundreds of other products as well.

Key Concepts

- » Handling disputes.
- » Intellectual property.
- » The Budweiser wars.
- » Global strategies.
- » Short-term versus long-term approaches – do your competitors think the same way as you do?
- » A glossary of global sales.

"And may you have a lawsuit and be in the right."

Romany curse

HANDLING DISPUTES

You've made the sale, but what happens if the customer says that the goods are not up to standard, the shipment arrives late, or any one of countless problems that might lead to the customer refusing to pay?

Experienced international firms say that it is almost never worth going to court. Even if you are successful, the costs, trouble, and delays will usually outweigh any benefit to be had from a legal victory. In India, for example, there is a backlog of more than 3 million commercial cases, and litigation can take over a decade. If the case is to be tried abroad, there is a high likelihood of losing even if the legal system is just – cultural differences lead to different interpretations, and neither judges nor juries are likely to be experienced in international transactions. The problems don't end there; negative publicity in the country may damage future business, collecting any money awarded may prove impossible, and trade secrets may be publicized in open court.

Many misunderstandings arise at contract stage from differences in the world's legal systems. There are four main legal traditions around the globe.

1 **Common law** – judgments are based on precedents, past rulings, interpretations of statutes, and customary principles. Common law is derived from English law and is used in the UK, the US (except for Louisiana), Canada (except for Quebec), and many countries formerly in the British Empire.
2 **Civil law** – judgments are based on a complex set of written rules that are intended to be all-inclusive. Civil law countries include Japan, most of Europe, and Latin America.
3 **Islamic law** – judgments are based on the interpretation of the Koran with the objective of social justice. The system upholds property rights, the sanctity of contracts, and the rights and duties of individuals. Business activities involved with gambling and alcohol are forbidden. It is forbidden to pay interest. The interpretation of Islamic law varies widely across the Muslim world, ranging from extreme fundamentalist to liberal. Turkey, for example, is a civil law

country with some Islamic laws, and allows the manufacture and sale of alcohol and the payment of interest.

4 **Communist law** – China and much of the former USSR are having to build legal systems from scratch to account for the private ownership of property. Laws tend to be vague and difficult to interpret, while enforcement and resolution mechanisms are ineffective. Eastern European countries such as Poland and the Czech Republic have reverted to their pre-communist legal codes.

An example of how disputes can easily arise where both parties sincerely feel that they are in the right is in the concept of acts of God. In common law, an act of God is an unusual natural calamity, such as an earthquake or a flood. Common law usually excuses non-performance of a contract caused by an act of God. In civil law, on the other hand, acts of God arising from natural events have a wider interpretation and also include unforeseeable human events, such as riots and strikes. Suppose water pipes burst during cold weather and damage goods stored in a warehouse. In common law, the vendor would be normally liable for non-performance on the grounds that frozen water pipes are predictable in harsh winter climates, while civil law courts might well define the event as an act of God and excuse the vendor.

Most international commercial disputes are settled privately. Sellers tend to take a long-term view, and consider whether they want to keep the customer for the future. If not, then it is often best to write off the loss and remember not to do business with that firm again. In other cases, friendly negotiation is effective. In many parts of the world, "face," "amour propre," and other notions of personal pride may prevent the customer from explaining the real reasons for the dispute. Calm, non-confrontational negotiation where you, the seller, make concessions often gives the customer a way of coming to terms without feeling humiliated. In Chinese culture, amicable negotiation is particularly highly valued, and the first step in any problem is to try to solve it peacefully through discussion.

If discussion fails, mediation can work. This is where a mutually chosen third party, such as a representative from a Chamber of Commerce or a firm in an allied industry, acts as a referee. Mediation can be arranged formally in some countries but is not usually legally binding, so if the parties sign an agreement it is useful to insert a clause stating that if the agreement is not kept the parties will go to official arbitration.

Arbitration is a more formal type of mediation where the two firms agree to abide by the arbiter's decision. Many organizations, including the International Chamber of Commerce (ICC), operate arbitration schemes across the world. In 2001, 566 new cases were registered with the ICC, mostly in Europe and North America. Amounts in dispute ranged from $50,000 to more than $1bn, with more than half being worth over $1mn.

Although cases are usually confidential, the ICC claims a high success rate. In one dramatic case in 2002, the ICC's International Maritime Bureau helped to negotiate the freeing of a ship, the *Panagia Tinou*, from pirates off the Somali coast. Carrying a multimillion-dollar cargo of fertilizers, the ship and its crew were held hostage for three weeks until an agreement was reached (it is not disclosed whether a ransom was paid) and were escorted to freedom by a German warship.

INTELLECTUAL PROPERTY

You are out selling a well-known brand abroad and you suddenly see pirate versions in the local stores at half the price. Your dreams of beating your sales target go up in smoke as you realize that the distributors you are visiting are quietly selling the pirate brand. What can you do?

Almost any valuable brand is worth pirating because of the premium on the price – designer clothing, fancy watches, software, cigarettes, packaged foods, medicines, books, movies, and vehicle spare parts are more expensive in their branded form. A counterfeit product of equivalent quality can be generally sold profitably for less. Pirates don't usually produce equivalent quality, but often copied products are remarkably good. A CD of the latest Hollywood blockbuster movie can be purchased for pennies in south-east Asia and is often a high-quality copy, despite the claims of the industry. Software costing hundreds of dollars in its branded form is widely pirated in Asia, selling for a few dollars; to the consumer, the benefits of getting bundles of the latest software far outweigh any possible glitches – they simply cannot afford to buy the real thing. A fake Rolex may only last for a few years, but it looks identical to a real Rolex and weighs the same; for those who wear Rolexes to show off rather than to tell the time, the 30-dollar cost of the "copy watch" may seem a good investment.

Foreign courts often sympathize with the pirates, especially in poor countries. For example, millions of people in India cannot afford to buy patented medicines and local officials find it difficult to see the moral argument of a multinational claiming that protecting its products is more important than allowing sick people access to treatment. In Russia, counterfeit medicines have 10% of the market, representing an estimated loss of $250mn a year. An estimated 40% of the counterfeit medicines are believed to be produced by Russia's largest legitimate pharmaceutical manufacturers, although they deny this. Local pharmaceuticals also produce "lookalike" products whose names and packaging are similar to competing Western brands. The French firm Aventis, a market leader in Russia, is said to have suffered the greatest losses, with six of its nine main products being widely counterfeited. One reason for the growth in piracy is an increase in prices following the introduction of VAT on drugs.

British and American firms frequently make the error of thinking that foreign courts will uphold their rights to their brand name on the grounds of prior use, but this is often not the case. Many civil law countries will favor the firm who first registered a trademark. Nike cannot use its name in Spain. "McDonald's" and "Microsoft" are locally owned trademarks in Jordan.

THE BUDWEISER WARS

There can only be one genuine Budweiser beer, right? Wrong – it all depends on what country you live in.

Budweis, a town in the Czech Republic, has been brewing beer since the Middle Ages. The name *Budweiser*, which means "from Budweis," was registered as a trademark in the 1920s, but had been used as a description of the Czech beer for centuries and received a royal warrant in the sixteenth century from the King of Bohemia entitling it to be called "the beer of kings." Budweis is the German name for the town, called Eeské Budejovice in Czech.

In 1876, immigrants set up a brewery in America, calling their product *Budweiser* and using the slogan "the king of beers," a play on the Czech beer's warranted title. A few years later, in 1895, Budvar, a brewery in Budweis, also started producing beer under the brand name *Budweiser*.

History was kinder to the US than Bohemia, and the American firm Anheuser-Busch grew into a massive organization, brewing over 26 million hectoliters of its product each year, compared with the 1 million hectoliters of the Czech firm. Budvar, however, has hugely increased production in recent years, transforming itself into a global organization. Although until recently US beer drinkers had never heard of the Czech beer, the two companies have been aware of each other for most of their existence. In 1939, for example, the year after Hitler annexed Czechoslovakia, Anheuser-Busch was able to persuade Budvar to sign an agreement not to market its beer as *Budweiser* in the US, a deal which many Czechs regard as having been made under duress.

Following the Velvet Revolution of 1989 when the communist government was overthrown, Anheuser-Busch immediately attempted to purchase Budvar. The newly capitalist Czechs have refused to privatize Budvar, however, on the grounds that it is part of the national heritage – Czechs drink a lot of beer – and Budvar is still owned by the Czech Ministry of Agriculture. Money is not the only issue – there are fears that Anheuser-Busch might convert the brewery to producing the American version of the beer, which many people regard as an inferior product.

For the last two decades, the firms have waged a vicious legal war with one another around the world for ownership of the brand name. In 2002, they were fighting some 40 lawsuits internationally. Apparently engaged in an unequal David-and-Goliath struggle, Budvar has scored some notable victories, all because of varying legal judgments in different countries.

» In the UK, both beers are allowed to be marketed under the same brand name.
» In Italy, the Czech beer can be sold as *Budweiser*, while the American beer is sold as *Bud*.
» In the US, the American firm controls the brand name, and the Czech version is marketed as *Czechvar*.

» South Korea, the fourth largest Asian market for beer, overruled an appeal by Anheuser-Busch and confirmed that the brand name belonged to Budvar in 2002.
» Germany, Portugal, Finland, Yugoslavia, the Baltic States, Greece, and Taiwan have ruled in favor of Budvar.
» Budvar markets its beer in Australia and New Zealand under the name *Budějovický Budvar*. In 2002, Anheuser-Busch failed in its attempt to prevent this name being used in Australia.

GLOBAL STRATEGIES

Globalization has not brought about a single, unified marketplace, but it has made it much easier for companies of all sizes to sell their products abroad. Increasingly, firms are realizing that the need for coherent global strategies applies not only to the largest multinationals, but to most international exporters.

The choices facing strategy-makers are very wide. For example, firms can be selective about which markets to enter. Smaller high-tech and luxury-goods firms often decide to focus on a small number of markets where the potential returns justify the effort to become established – all other markets are consciously ignored. Globalization means increased competition, however, so firms have to recognize that rivals may suddenly enter their own markets and also that they need to monitor developments in unserved territories where demand for their products may be growing.

The main features of a global strategy are as follows.

» **What, and how much, to standardize** – in Chapter 2 we saw that while standardization increases efficiency and reduces costs, local adaptation maximizes potential sales in a particular market. The rewards for standardization are often higher in industries involving very heavy investment in production, such as IT manufacturing. Small firms in particular may find it easier to customize their products for short runs.
» **Where to obtain resources** – innovative practices such as outsourcing telephone call centers and computer programing in India, and locating high-tech factories in remote parts of Malaysia, have been a

feature of the multinationals' policies in the 1990s. Smaller firms, such as Dyson, the UK maker of vacuum cleaners, have found it feasible to move production to the Far East to take advantage of lower labor costs – much to the astonishment of their British employees. Increasingly, senior executives in large international firms originate from all over the world, not just the home country. With fewer controls on the movement of money across borders, firms have more choice about where to borrow money, and what currency to borrow in. None of these procedures are as easy as they may sound, nor are they risk-free, but it is vital to consider every possibility of where to obtain resources. Firms that refuse, for example, to relocate their production centers to a cheaper country from sentimental or ideological reasons are likely to become uncompetitive.

» **Diversification** – the more markets a firm serves, the more potential there is for smoothing out fluctuations in demand, suppliers' prices, and so on. Part of a global strategy is to institute a mechanism to allow the company to respond quickly and "hedge" as needed. Communications and the flow of information to and from regional offices should be optimized to allow local managers to understand the reason for changes and respond in a constructive way. One manager in a global media firm, who has the responsibility of developing products solely for sale in his own region, complained in 2002 that "since the September 11 attack, sales in my territories have dropped – but so have our competitors'. Now head office won't allow us to produce any of the products I have worked so hard to develop. I know that if we introduce some of them now, we'll increase our market share substantially when the economies in this part of the world start to pick up again, but our bosses overseas won't listen." Perhaps this manager's bosses are following a sensible hedging strategy, but by failing to communicate, they have generated resentment among marketing and sales staff in the overseas subsidiaries with the greatest long-term growth potential.

» **Size does matter** – many smaller markets show little promise of large short-term profits, but that doesn't mean they should be ignored. By pursuing a break-even strategy in smaller markets, the resulting sales can still make a valuable contribution to reducing the production cost per unit.

» **Globalize your processes** – accounting, research, buying, human resources, finance, and marketing processes need to be internationalized. Many firms ensure that staff from different countries meet frequently at conferences to foster a sense of common purpose within the company.

SHORT-TERM VERSUS LONG-TERM APPROACHES – DO YOUR COMPETITORS THINK THE SAME WAY AS YOU DO?

Having a global outlook as opposed to the ethnocentric, export-based model is relatively new in international business. Stock market pressures on public companies in the US and UK contribute to a general focus on short-term profits, arguably at the expense of more valuable long-term gains. Japanese firms, on the other hand, are recognized as orientated towards the long term. But are the business principles they follow really so different? A three-year study of 90 large Japanese, US, and UK firms selling in the UK market (published in 1992) revealed some interesting insights

» Japanese firms market their products quite differently in different territories. Local subsidiaries have a great deal of autonomy in marketing decisions, but not in finance or production.
» The majority of the staff in the UK subsidiaries were British nationals, but the study still found marked differences between the three groups. More than half the US subsidiaries had an American marketing head, but only two Japanese firms had a Japanese one.
» Japanese subsidiaries in the UK were much more strategically ambitious than their rivals. While almost all US and UK firms focused on maintaining short-term profitability at all times, the Japanese felt that increasing market share was much more important.
» A fifth of UK firms stated that they made cheap, down-market products, but none of the other firms would admit to this.
» Some managers in US firms stated that their companies were not really committed to the UK market and the researchers felt that this was true of almost all of the US companies studied. One US manager said that "The USA is the largest market. Competitors, including the Japanese, will have to succeed in the US if they are to achieve

dominance. That is why our emphasis is on developing products for the US – we anticipate that they will serve the UK market as well." Japanese firms, on the other hand, seemed to attach importance to the UK market in its own right and as a springboard to other EU countries in the longer term. Although US firms had been in the UK for much longer, Japanese firms seem to have adapted far more.

» All the Japanese firms claimed that management–worker relations in the UK were satisfactory, but only 54% of US firms did so. The Western firms tended to have more complex hierarchies and poorer information systems, and were less market-focused.

» Across the three groups, the most successful companies all emphasized increasing market share over short-term profitability. They also spent more on in-house training, were more innovative, and had less rigid organizational structures. Some 58% of the successful companies were Japanese, but the non-Japanese companies that were successful were found to have a similar profile.[1]

A GLOSSARY OF GLOBAL SALES

Account management – the ongoing strategic direction of major clients' business.

Benefits – those things that a service does for or means to buyers, rather than the factual descriptions of it. (Compare with **Features**.)

Closing – action taken to gain a commitment to buy or proceed onwards towards the point where this can logically occur.

Cold-calling – approaches by any method (e.g. face to face or by telephone) to potential customers who have expressed no prior interest of any sort (i.e. who are "cold").

Competitor intelligence – information collected about competitive products and services, and their suppliers, which may specifically be used to improve the approach taken on a sales call.

Country of origin – in most countries, a label must indicate where the product was made, and this may influence customers' perception of its quality.

Cross-selling – the technique of selling a range of different services to an existing client.

Features – the factual things to be described about a service. (Compare with **Benefits**.)

Gatekeeper – someone who through their position (e.g. a secretary) can facilitate or deny access to a buyer.

Ego drive – Mayer and Greenberg's term for the internal motivational drive that makes a salesperson want to succeed.[2]

Empathy – Mayer and Greenberg's term for the ability to see things from other people's (i.e. customers') point of view and, importantly, be seen to do so.[3]

Field training – training or development activity undertaken away from any formal setting, out and about on territory.

Handling objections – the stage of sales presentations that is most highly interactive, where specific queries or challenges posed by potential buyers must be addressed, so as to keep the positive side of the case in the majority.

Influencers – people who, while not having exclusive authority to buy, influence the buyer (e.g. through their recommendation).

Key/major/national/global accounts – terms used to describe very large customers to whom the supplier gives special sales attention. The sales force usually works as a team, making many calls on different individuals in the purchasing firm before finally achieving a close. Profit margins may be agreed in advance, so the focus of sales calls tends to be on quality-related issues.

Need identification – the process of asking questions to discover exactly what clients want, and why, as a basis for deciding how to pitch a sales presentation.

Negotiation – a different, though closely allied, skill to selling and very important in some kinds of business. (See also Chapters 2 and 8 in the ExpressExec title *Negotiating*.)

On-the-job training – field training and development activity, often in the form of joint calls with a manager.

Pie system – a structured way of managing the spread of customers and prospects around a sales territory.

Proposal – normally implies a written document, one including the price but more than a quotation, which spells out the case and most often reflects a clear brief that has been given or established.

Prospecting – the search for new contacts who may be potential clients, by such wide-ranging means as cold-calling and desk research.

Qualifying prospects – research or action to produce information demonstrating that "cold" prospects are "warm."

Sales aids – items, information, or even other people used during a sales conversation to enhance what is said.

Sales audit – an occasional systematic review of all aspects of sales activity and its management to identify areas needing improvement, or working well and needing extension. The process recognizes the inherent dynamic nature of sales.

Sales productivity – the sales equivalent of productivity in an area, the focus being on efficiencies that maximize the amount of time spent with customers (rather than traveling, writing reports, etc.). It focuses on ratios, and touches on anything that increases sales success, however measured.

Territory – the area covered by an individual salesperson. It is usually, but not always, geographic.

NOTES

1 Doyle, P., Saunders, J., & Wong, V. (1992) "Competition in global markets: a case study of American and Japanese competition in the British market." *Journal of International Business Studies*, third quarter, pp. 419-42.

2 Mayer, D. & Greenberg, H.M. (1964) "What makes a good salesman." *Harvard Business Review*, pp. 119-25.

3 *Ibid.*

Resources

» Key books.
» Key Websites.
» Further reading.

Here is a basic guide to some of the key books and Websites to consult when beginning to get to grips with global sales.

KEY BOOKS

Relentless: The Japanese way of marketing

by J.K. Johansson and I. Nonaka (New York, HarperBusiness, 1997)

After several years of weak economic conditions, there has been a general perception that the so-called "Japanese miracle" has stalled. Not so, however, since Japanese companies have managed to sustain their positions and are now poised to strengthen their prominence in the world marketplace, particularly in the exports of automobiles, consumer and industrial electronics, and steel. In their new book *Relentless: The Japanese way of marketing*, Johny Johansson and Ikujiro Nonaka suggest that this sustained dominance is due to the method of Japanese marketing. Their main thesis is that Western companies should integrate the Japanese method with Western techniques. Conversely, the authors rigorously probe Japanese marketing philosophy, and stress the need for Japan's business leaders to integrate certain aspects of Western marketing philosophy.

The authors explore American marketing approaches in depth and suggest that they are imbued with notions of "rugged individualism" and professionalism, and over-reliant on abstract study, statistics, and theories. A sharp distinction is made from Japanese marketing techniques with no "professional" marketers, fully inclusive marketing participation, and an alternative but enhanced front-line seller–customer relationship, providing them with a direct understanding of the customer's needs and promoting optimal customer service. Crucially it is demonstrated that this understanding equips the Japanese with the essential skills of "intuitive strategy," enabling them to develop rapid, flexible, and adaptable marketing plans without the years of research invested in Western strategy development. Moreover, the authors demonstrate that accurate customer understanding also propels product development with a speed and flexibility that enables new markets to be generated by the products per se.

A Nation of Salesmen: The tyranny of the market and the subversion of culture
by E. Shorris (New York, Norton, 1994)

Drawing from his long experiences as an advertising executive and consultant to major corporations, Earl Shorris's *A Nation of Salesmen* addresses the concept of the sale comprehensively. The author's principal thesis is that selling has become the determinant activity in the US. Part One examines definitions and the history of the sale. This aspect of the book is particularly disappointing (and hard to swallow), since the author generates a series of fictional anecdotes that are difficult to reconcile with the dynamics of global sales in the twenty-first century. For instance, Shorris begins literally "at the beginning," portraying the typical salesperson as the serpent in the Garden of Eden. Part Two is dedicated to the concept of selling in the US per se, and suggests that the nation became oversold – everyone from your local doctor to Bill Clinton made the sale! Part Three examines the impact of sales on post-World War II American society. It is contended that selling has caused individuals to become self-reflective concerning aspects of their personal and social life (notably freedom and dignity).

Shorris combines several principles of philosophy, politics, applied economics, and anecdotal fiction with his own first-hand observations and interviews of a wide array of salespeople, in order to illustrate how the US became a nation of salesmen. Despite its obvious weaknesses, this book does approach sales in a novel, stimulating, and thought-provoking way; as such, it is a must for every professional engaged in sales and marketing.

Management Challenges for the 21st Century
by P.F. Drucker (New York, HarperBusiness, 1999)

Peter Drucker's influence on the course of business in the twentieth century was profound. In this new work, the author examines the profound social and economic changes occurring today and considers how management (as opposed to government or free markets) should orient itself to address these new realities. The author singles out five social and political aspects that he believes are destined to shape business policies in the near future on an unprecedented scale – the collapsing birth rate of the developed world; changes in the distribution of disposable income; a redefinition of corporate performance; global competitiveness; and the growing disparity between economic and political reality.

Drucker also examines leadership requirements. For instance, he suggests that change cannot be managed; rather, one can only be ahead of it. The characteristics of the so-called "new information revolution" are also assessed; it is argued that the focus should be on the meaning of information as opposed to the technology that gathers it. Drucker acknowledges the productivity of the knowledge worker, emphasizing the need to view them as capital assets, not costs (unlike manual workers). Finally, emphasis is laid on the new demands that will be placed on the individual knowledge worker who will outlive the organizations that employ them, putting responsibility on individuals to manage themselves. This work is a prerequisite for any professional engaged in the business management sphere – CEOs, managers, and knowledge workers alike.

Sales Force Management, 7th edn

by M.W. Johnston and G.W. Marshall (Chicago, Irwin/McGraw-Hill, 2001)

Now under the authorship of Mark Johnston and Greg Marshall, this text represents one of the most comprehensive discussions of sales management issues in print. The volume is essentially a research- and theory-based text. The theoretical roots of sales management are defined and blended with examples and applications from contemporary industry. The 7th edition text contains the welcome addition of three new themes – innovation, leadership, and technology. The format of this book lends itself to a variety of teaching approaches, from the lecture and discussion method to case-oriented teaching. This work represents an admirably strong base in sales management. Moreover, its research and theory emphasis combine to make it the definitive benchmark book in sales management.

Managing Cultural Differences, 5th edn

by P.R. Harris and R.T. Moran (Houston, Gulf Publishing, 2000)

The best-selling guide by Philip R. Harris and Robert T. Moran demonstrates how to develop the cross-cultural expertise essential to succeed in sales amid a world of rapid and profound economic, political, and cultural changes. While retaining its traditional place as a rich source of information on the dynamics of culture and business, the 5th edition presents several innovations. There is a new chapter dedicated to the topic of women in global business and an emphasis on effective cross-cultural strategies and policies. These vital resource topics are designed to aid the global salesperson take advantage of expanding international markets, enhance cross-cultural business communication skills, master business protocol, and generate a successful multicultural management program.

An excellent feature of the text is the introduction of lucid mini-case histories, illustrations, and country profiles. The text offers guidelines to improve leadership skills in many fields, including globalization, communications, negotiations, strategic alliances, cultural changes, cultural synergy, and diversity in the workplace. The 5th edition contains a reorganized companion instructor's guide and will thus serve as an invaluable tool in the academic sphere. This latest edition of *Managing Cultural Differences* will strengthen the position of the guide as the leading source of information on the dynamics of culture and business.

KEY WEBSITES

Designing the sales force

www.terralign.com The TerrAlign Group site provides a useful insight into the design of global sales forces (expatriates, local nationals, and third-country nationals) using US models; in particular, the company has provided tools to help international firms create balanced territories and find optimal locations for sales offices in Canada, Mexico, and Australia.

www.kornferry.com. All aspects of recruiting marketing and sales personnel are covered on the site of Korn/Ferry International, the largest international executive search firm.

Global sales and legal issues

www.law.com The Law.com site contains a variety of reports, treaties, laws, and other information on legal issues regarding international trade.

www.lexmercatoria.net The Lex Mercatoria site contains in-depth coverage of international trade law, including conciliation and arbitration.

Global sales and cultural awareness

www.culturegrams.com In global sales, the need to adapt to local cultures is of paramount importance. This site contains information on various cultural traits, gestures, holidays, languages, religions, and issues.

www.milken-inst.org The Milken Institute site provides a useful comparison of technology, economics, and education systems across countries.

www.webofculture.com The Web of Culture site provides a variety of data on cultural dimensions such as language, gestures, and religion for a large number of countries.

Multinational market regions and market groups

Europe

www.europa.eu.int/index-en.htm This site gives a detailed and up-to-date account of the multinational market regions and market groups within Europe – the European Economic Community (EEC), the European Union (EU), the European Free Trade Area (EFTA) and the European Economic Area (EEA).

The Americas

www.mac.doc.gov NAFTA is a comprehensive trade agreement that addresses, and in most cases improves, all aspects of doing business within North America. The elimination of trade and investment barriers among Canada, Mexico, and the US creates one of the largest and richest markets in the world. A complete description of NAFTA structure and provisions may be found on this site.

www.mercosur.org/english/ The Southern Cone Free Trade Area (Mercosur) is the second largest common-market agreement in Latin America after NAFTA. The treaty calls for a common market that would eventually allow for the free movement of goods, capital, labor, and services among the member countries, with a uniform external tariff.

www.oas.org/ The Organization of American States home page provides detailed information on all Latin American trade agreements including the Andean Common Market (ANCOM), the Central American Common Market (CACM), the Caribbean Community and Common Market (CARICOM), and the Latin American Integration Association (LAIA).

Asian Pacific Rim

www.aseansec.org/ This is the home page of the primary multinational trade group in Asia (ASEAN), including Brunei, Indonesia, Malaysia, the Philippines, Singapore, Thailand, Vietnam, Myanmar, and Laos. Its objectives are economic integration and cooperation through complementary industry programs, preferential trading, guaranteed-member access to markets throughout the region, and harmonized investment incentives.

Government organizations

www.stat-usa.gov STAT-USA/Internet is the most important source of data on the Internet. STAT-USA, a service of the US Department of Commerce, produces and distributes the most extensive government-sponsored business, economic, and trade information databases in the world today (for a nominal subscription fee), including the National Trade Data Bank, the Economic Bulletin Board, and Global Business Procurement Opportunities.

www.ita.doc.gov The site of the International Trade Administration, another service of the US Department of Commerce, provides export assistance, including information about trade events, trade statistics, tariffs and taxes, marketing research, and so on.

www.usatradeonline.gov The USA Trade Online site provides import and export information on more than 18,000 commodities (on a user-must-subscribe basis).

www.imf.org The International Monetary Fund (IMF) site provides information about the IMF and international banking and finance.

www.wto.org The World Trade Organization site provides information about its operations.

www.oecd.org The Organization of Economic Cooperation and Development (OECD) provides information about OECD policies and associated data for 29 member countries.

www.jetro.go.jp The Japan External Trade Organization is the best source for data on the Japanese market.

Non-government organizations (NGOs)

www.euromonitor.com Euromonitor is a company providing a variety of data and reports on international trade and marketing.

www.doingbusiness.com Ernst & Young's Doing Business around the World series has been converted to a folio infobase format for Internet viewing. The series provides country profiles that survey the investment climate, forms of business organization, and business and accounting practices in more than 40 countries.

www.ipl.orgref/RR/static/bus4700.html The Internet Public Library provides Internet addresses for dozens of sources of trade data worldwide.

http://iserve.wtca.org The World Trade Centers Association provides information about services provided by the world trade centers in the US, including export assistance, trade leads, training programs, and trade missions.

www.worldtrademag.com The *World Trade* magazine provides online its annual resource guide to products, goods, and services for international trade.

University-based Websites

http://globaledge.msu.edu/ibrd/ibrd.asp The site of the Michigan State University Center for International Business Education and Research.

www.lib.berkeley.edu/BUSI/bbg18.html This site is maintained by the University of California at Berkeley and contains international business information.

FURTHER READING

Aigner, D.J. (2000) "The 2000 Orange County executive survey," University of California, Graduate School of Management, 28.

Allinson, C.W. & Hayes, J. (2000) "Cross-national differences in cognitive style: implications for management." *International Journal of Human Resource Management*, 11(1), 161–170.

Anstead, M. (1999) "Marketing that loses a little in translation: global adverts face cultural pitfalls." *Daily Telegraph*, August 19.

Axtell, R.E. (1995) *Do's and Taboos of Using English around the World*. John Wiley & Sons, New York.

Baker, S. (1992) "Europe swoons for voice on the Net." *Business Week*, May 1, 192.

Bjerke, B. (2000) *Business Leadership and Culture: National management styles in the global economy*. Edward Elgar Publishing, Northampton, MA.

Boscariol, J.W. (1999) "An anatomy of a Cuban pyjama crisis." *Law and Policy in International Business*, 439.

Clarke, S. & Metalina, T. (2000) "Training in the new private sector in Russia." *International Journal of Human Resource Management*, 11(1), 19–36.

DeSchields Jr., O.W. & de los Santos, G. (2000) "Salesperson's accent as a global issue." *Thunderbird International Review*, 42(1), 29–46.

Forster, N. (2000) "The myth of the international manager." *International Journal of Human Resource Management*, 11(1), 126–142.

Foster, D.A. (2000) *The Global Etiquette Guide to Asia*. John Wiley & Sons, New York.

Greimel, H. (2000) "Religion imposes limits on devout Muslims' wallets." *Dallas Morning News*, April 21.

Hodgson, J.D., Sano, Y., & Graham, J.L. (2000) *Doing Business in the New Japan*. Rowman & Littlefield, Boulder, CO.

Hofstede, G. (1991) *Culture and Organizations*. McGraw-Hill, London.

Huff, L.C. & Dana, L.A. (2000) "A model of managerial response to sales promotions: a four-country analysis." *Journal of Global Marketing*, **13**(3), 7–28.

Hussain Ali Jafri, S. & Margolis, L.S. (1999) "The treatment of usury in the Holy Scriptures," *Thunderbird International Business Review*, **41**(4/5), 371.

Mandell, M. (1999) "Safer traveling." *World Trade*, December, 48–52.

Marcks, E. (2000) "English law in early Hong Kong: colonial law as a means for control and liberation." *Texas International Law Journal*, April, 265.

Money, R.B., Gilly, M.C., & Graham, J.L. (1998) "National culture and referral behavior in the purchase of industrial services in the United States and Japan." *Journal of Marketing*, **62**(4), 76–87.

Money, R.B., Gilly, M.C., & Graham, J.L. (1999) "Sales performance, pay, and job satisfaction: tests of a model using data collected in the US and Japan." *Journal of International Business Studies*, **30**(1), 149–172.

Neelankavil, J.P., Mathur, A., & Zhang, Y. (2000) "Determinants of managerial performance: a cross-cultural comparison of the perceptions of middle-level managers in four countries." *Journal of International Business Studies*, **31**(1), 121–140.

Pornpitakpan, C. (2000) "Trade in Thailand: a three-way cultural comparison." *Business Horizons*, March–April, 61–70.

Rasmusson, E. (2000) "Going global with CRM." *Sales & Marketing Management*, **152**(3), 96–98.

Rykken, R. (2000) "Square pegs: hiring the wrong person for an overseas assignment can lead to disaster." *Global Business*, 58–61.

Smith, A. (1993 [1776]) *An Inquiry into the Nature and Causes of the Wealth of Nations*, Book IV (ed. E. Cannan). Modern Library, New York.

Song, X.M., Xie, J., & Dyer, B. (2000) "Antecedents and consequences of marketing managers' conflict-handling behaviors." *Journal of Marketing*, January, 50–66.

Sowinski, L.L. (2000) "Customer relationship software." *World Trade*, 70–71.

Ten Steps to Making Global Sales Work

Key opportunities and issues in global sales, including:

» Using local people
» Packaging and labelling problems
» Coping with cultural differences
» Adapt your product!
» Resolving disputes
» Winning hearts and minds

1. USE LOCAL PEOPLE

The glory days of the expatriate middle manager are over. As countries around the world have raised standards of education, recruiting local managers has become easier; it is also far less expensive than exporting a home-country manager, complete with spouse and children. Many countries actively resist introducing foreign managers except where it can be shown that their presence is essential. While experienced firms are familiar with the issue, many new exporters make very old-fashioned assumptions about how to staff foreign operations. A foreign office will usually need one or two permanent expatriate staff to supply expertise that is not available locally, and also to act as a conduit of ideas to and from the home base. Specialized super-salespeople often cover many countries, arriving to work on important prospects for a short period in conjunction with their local colleagues. This solution is a practical one for many firms, and has the virtue of having evolved naturally in response to the international business environment. New entrants frequently fail to appreciate the high levels of motivation among local people. Providing a career path that allows them to go abroad for a period is an added incentive.

2. ASSESS THE EXTENT OF ANTI-COMPETITIVE PRACTICES

As in other walks of life, it is natural to try to defend a territory from interlopers in business. At home, regulation may keep the playing field relatively level, but internationally there are many industries and markets where a few established insiders collude to prevent new competitors from succeeding. Most of us know of only a few examples of this strategy because it tends to be secretive even where it is legal. OPEC is the most famous cartel, and international shipping cartels are the longest-lived, but cartel behavior is very widespread. Examining whether there are restrictive practices should be an essential step in preparing to enter any new market; don't assume that things will be just the same as they are at home.

Cartels don't necessarily last for very long. Private agreements to fix prices, for example, are difficult to police when every member has an incentive to cheat. As markets fluctuate and develop, cartels tend to break down, often recurring again and again in some industries when warranted by market conditions. Don't assume that an existing barrier to entry will remain for ever – the chances are that opportunities will arise in the future.

3. ANALYZE WHETHER YOUR PRODUCT IS RIGHT FOR E-COMMERCE

Selling on the Internet is barely out of its infancy, and it cannot be known how it will develop in the future. Don't forget that for billions of people, simply using a keyboard with Roman letters is a major barrier, and translation of a Website into local languages will not make it universally accessible. Use the medium's advantages to work in your favor – such as the scope for detailed information, rapid updating, and visual aids – and analyze your products closely. Some products seem much better suited to the Internet than others, largely because of customers' requirements. As a salesperson, you know your market; list the reasons why people buy, and consider whether you can satisfy them better by offering facilities for online sales or information. Overall, Internet advertising has proved a failure so far, largely because of misguided attempts to "push" ads at viewers who do not want them. Remember that the appeal of the Internet to the user has a lot to do with increased freedom of access to information; for many users, the last thing they want is an inappropriate, invasive ad. With a few notable exceptions, online sales are not a stand-alone channel, but work as part of an integrated online/offline approach. Expensive facilities such as call centers may be essential to convince customers that their orders really have been received; Dell's online "Order Status" feature, for example, serves to allay the fears of online purchasers. Cannibalization of existing customers is a real problem, but some industries have coped by providing more specialized services online to attract a different type of client.

4. BE PREPARED FOR PACKAGING AND LABELING PROBLEMS

Governments everywhere generate a torrent of new regulations on packaging each year. Some firms, such as Castrol, have instituted highly sophisticated computer networks to enable them to keep track of new requirements, enabling them to minimize the potential losses. Translation must always be accurate, and local offices should have input into the system. For example, in the UK and the US, it is common to use the word "America" to refer to the US only, but this usage causes grave offence in Latin American countries who rightly feel that they are also part of the two American continents.

Health scares often cause rule changes, and not only for food and drugs; even spurious stories that some material is carcinogenic, for instance, can lead to rushed legislation intended to pacify public fears.

5. THINK ABOUT CULTURAL DIFFERENCES

Geert Hofstede's four dimensions for analyzing cultural traits is just one of many models scholars are using to study the way that different societies tend to behave in business. There are sometimes claims that these differences do not exist, or are irrelevant, but this is not a view with much currency in successful firms. Hofstede's model yields valuable insights because it shows how very different societies may have a characteristic in common – Taiwan and Ecuador having low "individualism," for example. It is useful to employ such models as a common language when deciding how to approach a particular market. Non-verbal behavior is particularly interesting; how close you stand to the other person, whether or not you touch, whether you stare at the face, and so on vary very widely. The "wrong" behavior can be interpreted as very rude, and because much non-verbal behavior is perceived below the level of awareness, it can lead to hostility without anyone knowing why.

6. REMEMBER THAT SMALL FIRMS DON'T HAVE TO SELL DIRECT

Setting up an overseas operation can take years and a sizeable investment, so it is out of the question for the majority of smaller firms. Instead, they must make some arrangement with a local intermediary – the challenge is in how to grab market share and promote aggressively when working at arm's length.

Check Point, a small Israeli firm profiled in Chapter 7, invented "firewalls," the computer security software for the Internet and other networks. Although it controls some 60% of the firewall business, it uses no direct salespeople in the US, its key market. Instead, it has developed very close relationships with intermediaries, providing training and support, and has worked hard to promote a positive, high-quality image in a notoriously fickle industry. By establishing a quality standard, OPSEC, Check Point has made buying decisions much easier for customers while furthering its own cause; intermediaries say that OPSEC is a vital part of their salespeople's armory of benefits.

7. ADAPT YOUR PRODUCT

Cultural, environmental, and regulatory factors force most industries to adapt their products for specific markets. While some transnational homogeneous markets exist, few can be said to be truly global. See this as an opportunity to defeat the competition, not as a burden. Sensitive adaptation of a product may be greatly appreciated by local customers. In poorer countries there is a high demand for "Western" products, but consumers cannot afford to buy them in standard quantities; many firms have introduced inexpensive small packages, such as single-use shampoo sachets, to reach these customers. Product positioning varies too – what may be a downmarket product in one country may be the preferred choice of the affluent in another.

When you translate instructions, check that they will be properly understood by the people who will use them; Spanish translations, for example, have to be tailored carefully for specific countries, because the meaning of many words varies across the Spanish-speaking world.

Climate and environment have a powerful effect on many products that "armchair" marketing decisions made at home may ignore. Local market research and input from local colleagues are essential.

8. AVOID INTERNATIONAL DISPUTES AND LEGAL BATTLES

If the stakes are very high, as in the Budweiser case described in Chapter 8, it may be worth the vast expense of waging a global legal war, but for run-of-the-mill local disputes the consensus is "Stay out of court." Many genuine misunderstandings occur because of conceptual differences between common law and civil law jurisdictions. For example, "acts of God" are defined differently, and a firm's duties and obligations are very differently conceived. When making a deal overseas, make sure that you are familiar enough with local practices to be alert to potential problems. Contention can easily arouse xenophobic feelings in the foreign country, from the richest to the poorest, and foreign firms need to be sensitive to local attitudes. In Muslim countries it is particularly important to respect religious views, and it is sometimes difficult to distinguish between genuine offences and opportunistic claims – however, a firm that employs locals and has long-standing relationships with the authorities can usually obtain protection and justice. Protecting trademarks and other intellectual property rights continues to be a major problem, exacerbated by attitudes in some countries that piracy is simply a way of leveling the commercial playing field. Pressure through trade organizations and diplomatic channels has had some effect, but with the premiums on some well-known or patented brands at very high levels, pirates do have some justification for their activities. Piracy is an issue that will run and run for the foreseeable future.

9. INCREASE MARKET SHARE OR SHORT-TERM PROFITS?

US firms are often accused of being unduly concerned with short-term profitability in overseas markets, yet in China, where most foreign firms are losing money, their presence is justified on long-term grounds. Japan is praised for seeking long-term market share at the expense of short-term profits, yet in the early postwar period it had a reputation for producing shoddy goods. The issue is probably not a cultural one; companies' approaches do change over time and are always influenced by how they are financed (US stock markets had a fad for short-termism in the 1980s and 1990s), the economic circumstances of their home country, and so on. Multinationals are still rooted in their country of origin and may possibly always remain so. Despite the rhetoric, all firms do tend to see the world through parochial filters. Don't expect your firm to be completely globally enlightened and objective!

10. FOCUS ON WINNING HEARTS AND MINDS

You may think your firm is simply selling a fine product or service, but in a foreign market people may see you as a tool of a hostile foreign government or the WTO; an alien religion; a disease; or any one of the bugbears that appear from time to time in every society. A proactive stance often works, such as McDonald's remarkably successful campaign in Serbia to show that it was sharing in the suffering caused by the NATO bombing of 1999. This phenomenon is not confined to war-torn or developing countries – it also appears in the US and European countries in response to a perceived threat, such as French activism against British beef, or US resentment at the success of Japanese firms.

Cultivating relationships, showing that you are there to stay, proving that you contribute to the community (for example, by sponsoring local events), adapting products to local tastes, and generally following a "good neighbor" policy reaps dividends; the great mistake is to become defensive or hostile.

KEY LEARNING POINTS

1 Expect to use local people for the majority of tasks in any overseas market.

2 Recognize that collusion between existing market players may be a substantial barrier to entry.

3 Some products are better suited for e-commerce than others. Is yours really one of them? Do you have Websites in foreign languages?

4 If a foreign market only requires a simple sticker in its own language as part of the label, don't think it will stay that way. Imposing new packaging rules is a bureaucratic growth industry across the world.

5 Cultural differences are real and important, so study the academic literature.

6 Direct selling is the most expensive and most rewarding method, but smaller firms can rarely afford to undertake it abroad. Look for ways to work in close partnership with local intermediaries.

7 Adapting your product is the norm, not the exception, internationally. Look for ways to enhance the product's local appeal by customizing it.

8 Avoid legal battles with overseas customers.

9 There seems to be no "right" answer to the question of whether to sacrifice short-term profits for long-term market share. Much depends on what the firm can afford, and what its other long-term objectives are. As a tactical weapon, it may be effective to do the opposite of what the competition is doing.

10 Be a good neighbor in your host countries and show that you are there for the long term. Nobody wants a foreign shark – there are always far too many local ones already!

Frequently Asked Questions

Q1: What are country-of-origin effects?
A: See Chapter 2, Country-of-origin effects.

Q2: Do international cartels really exist, and are they legal?
A: See Chapter 3, throughout.

Q3: What consumer products are the best-sellers online?
A: See Chapter 4, The consumer markets.

Q4: How much is the metric system used in the US?
A: See Chapter 5, The metric system.

Q5: How different are distribution channels in different countries?
A: See Chapter 5, Best practice varies across the globe.

Q6: Do I need ISO?

A: See Chapter 5, ISO 9000.

Q7: Are global brands really accepted everywhere?

A: See Chapter 6, Adapting the product.

Q8: How can a small firm in a foreign country dominate a US market for a product?

A: See Chapter 7, Check Point – mastering indirect sales.

Q9: Do global brands adapt to local tastes?

A: See Chapter 7, McDonald's – the mixed blessing of success.

Q10: What's the difference between civil law and common law, and does it matter?

A: See Chapter 8, Handling disputes.

Index

EXPRESSEXEC –
BUSINESS THINKING AT YOUR FINGERTIPS

ExpressExec is a 12-module resource with 10 titles in each module. Combined they form a complete resource of current business practice. Each title enables the reader to quickly understand the key concepts and models driving management thinking today.

Available from:
www.expressexec.com

Customer Service Department
John Wiley & Sons Ltd
Southern Cross Trading Estate
1 Oldlands Way, Bognor Regis
West Sussex, PO22 9SA
Tel: +44(0)1243 843 294
Fax: +44(0)1243 843 303
Email: cs-books@wiley.co.uk

9 781841 124551